Finding Hidden Treasures

Ron Price

Finding Hidden Treasures

ISBN: 0-937539-89-9

Designed by PG Studio

Published by
Executive Books
206 West Allen Street
Mechanicsburg, PA 17055

Printed in the United States of America

Acknowledgements

First, I am very grateful for all the people who have assisted in the creation of *Finding Hidden Treasures*:

- Jesse Price, Parson Ge and the staff at PG Studio, for their patience and professionalism in the layout, design, and printing.

- Rachel Derowitsch, for her terrific editing skills and Sherri Linsenbach, for the indexing.

- Pamela Price, for her assistance with diamonds of the body.

- A special thanks to Tim Eckstrom, who picked up extra responsibilities in our business so I could dedicate more time to completing this project.

- A special thanks to everyone who encouraged me along the way by showing interest in the final project.

Second, I am grateful for a lifetime of personal heroes who have taught me the importance of searching for hidden treasures. They are too many to name in this space, but many of them are quoted throughout this book and many more have inspired me by the example they set through their lives.

Third, I am grateful to my family, who has paid the highest price for this book—the continuous sacrifices they have made through the years so that I could keep going on new treasure hunts.

Finally, I am most grateful to you, the reader, because my payday will only come if this book provides some direction for you to discover your own hidden treasures.

Ron Price
December 2003

To our six children,

Jesse, Lucas, Nicholas, Daniel, Emily, and Alex,

who will discover and use hidden treasures far greater than
we can ever imagine.

And to their mother, Pamela, who through tireless years of
pursuing the greatest calling on earth shaped their
diamonds within.

Table of Contents

Introduction

Frank and Jim met every day for lunch out on the patio behind their office. They both brought lunch from home, and Jim was constantly impressed by the variety of his wife's lunch creations. Frank, on the other hand, would open his lunch box day after day and begin complaining, "I can't believe it—I hate peanut butter and jelly sandwiches." This went on for days and weeks, until one day it finally happened. Apparently, Frank had a bad morning, because instead of just complaining about his peanut butter and jelly sandwiches after removing them from his lunch box, he smashed the sandwiches with his fist, threw them down on the patio, stomped on them, and walked back into the office building. Jim was stunned and wasn't quite sure what to do. After finishing his lunch, he picked up the smashed sandwiches and deposited them in the trash can before returning to his office. But he couldn't forget Frank's anger. So when the afternoon break came, he gingerly entered Frank's office and sat down in the chair across the desk.

"Frank, if you don't like peanut butter and jelly sandwiches, why don't you tell your wife not to make them anymore?"

Frank responded, "Don't bring my wife into this—I make my own sandwiches!"

It's a funny, almost absurd story, but all too often it is an accurate picture of how we live our lives. We complain and grumble and blame, when we are the ones making our own sandwiches. *Finding Hidden Treasures* is about changing the stuff we use to make our lunch.

In *Success through a Positive Mental Attitude*, Napoleon Hill and W. Clement Stone wrote, "It is customary for a man to share a part of his tangible wealth with his loved ones as he goes through life, or he may do so in his will. This world would be a better world to live in if each person would leave, as an inheritance to posterity, the philosophy and know-how that brought him happiness, physical, mental and spiritual health and wealth."

Over the past thirty-five years, I have been privileged to work in diverse careers, including live theatre, truck tire retreading, church ministry, personal coaching, organizational consulting, nutrition/wellness education, and international sales and marketing. Through these varied careers, one theme has driven me to learn and grow: that each of us has been given infinite potential that is never exhausted or fully utilized. These "hidden treasures" provide immeasurable opportunities to explore, discover, achieve, and enjoy life. Throughout life we become who we are, not based on the circumstances or people around us, but on how we utilize these treasures within.

Fortunately, this book is only half completed—the rest must be finished in the reading. My desire is that *Finding Hidden Treasures* will spark original thinking in you and serve as a catalyst for your own adventure and treasure hunt. Because half of the job is in the reading, I suggest three different ways to approach your journey through this book:

1. For entertainment purposes. You can skim through this quickly to see if anything catches your interest, maybe pick it up and read a chapter when you are bored or waiting for someone, or just read the table of contents and last chapter so you can check it off as another book for the shelf.

2. To influence your thinking. If you use a highlighter while you read and underline a key sentence that got you thinking here and there, maybe read a chapter or two at night before going to sleep, there may be a gem or two that will help enrich your life.

3. To change your destiny. If you want your investment to reap returns never matched by the stock market, the real estate industry, or any other pursuit of wealth, use this book as a shovel to dig up treasures beyond your wildest dreams. Use the highlighter as you read, read each chapter at least three times in a week, complete all of the actions steps at the end of each chapter, and get involved in a book study group to help

you dig deeper in your hunt for hidden treasures.

However you decide to use this book in your life, remember: you're the one making the sandwiches, and you're the one who gets to eat them!

Ron Price
December 2003

Chapter 1
Russell Conwell's "Acres of Diamonds"

Russell Conwell is one of my heroes. He served in the American Civil War, worked as a lawyer and journalist, and finally settled for a career as the pastor of Baptist Temple and founder of Temple College (now Temple University). He gave the speech "Acres of Diamonds" more than 6,000 times, probably making it the most repeated live speech in American history. The speech, which lasted longer than ninety minutes, is full of vivid examples about how often we are blind to the wealth of opportunities before us.

Below is the opening story of this speech:

> Ladies and gentlemen: The title of this lecture originated away back in 1869. When going down the Tigris River, we hired a guide from Baghdad to show us down to the Arabian Gulf. That guide whom we employed resembled the barbers we find in America. That is, he resembled the barbers in certain mental characteristics. He thought it was not only his duty to guide us down the river, but also to entertain us with stories; curious and weird, ancient and modern, strange and familiar; many of them I have forgotten, and I am glad I have. But there was one which I recall tonight. The guide grew irritable over my lack of appreciation, and as he led my camel by the halter he introduced his story by saying, "This is a tale I reserve for my *particular friends.*" So I then gave him my close attention. He told me that there once lived near the shore of the River Indus, toward which we were then traveling, an ancient Persian by the name of Al Hafed. He said that Al Hafed owned a large farm, with orchards, grain fields and gardens; that he had money at interest, had a beautiful wife and lovely children, and was a wealthy and contented man. Contented because he was wealthy, and wealthy because he was contented.

One day there visited this old Persian farmer one of those ancient Buddhist priests, one of the wise men of the East, who sat down by Al Hafed's fireside and told the old farmer how this world was made. He told him that this world was once a great bank of fog, and that the Almighty thrust His finger into this bank of fog, and began slowly to move his finger around, and then increased the speed of his finger until he whirled this bank of fog into a solid ball of fire; and as it went rolling through the universe, burning its way through other banks of fog, it condensed the moisture, until it fell in floods of rain upon the heated surface of the world, and cooled the outward crust; then the internal fires, bursting the cooling crust, threw up the mountains, and the hills, and the valleys of this wonderful world of ours.

"And," said the old priest, "if this internal melted mass burst forth and cooled very quickly it became granite, if it cooled more slowly, it became copper; if it cooled less quickly, silver; less quickly, gold; and after gold, diamonds were made." Said the old priest, "A diamond is a congealed drop of sunlight." That statement is literally true.

And the old priest said another very curious thing. He said that a diamond was the last and the highest of God's mineral creations, as a woman is the last and highest of God's animal creations. That is the reason, I suppose, why the two have such a liking for each other.

The old priest told Al Hafed if he had a diamond the size of his thumb, he could purchase a dozen farms like his. "And," said the priest, "if you had a handful of diamonds, you could purchase the county, and if you had a mine of diamonds you could purchase kingdoms, and place your children upon thrones, through the influence of your great wealth."

Al Hafed heard all about the diamonds that night, and went to bed a poor man. He wanted a whole mine of diamonds. Early in the morning he sought the priest and awoke him. Well, I know, by experience, that a priest is very cross when awakened early in the morning.

Al Hafed said: "Will you tell me where I can find diamonds?"

The priest said: "Diamonds? What do you want of diamonds?"

Said Al Hafed: "I want to be immensely rich."

"Well," said the priest, "if you want diamonds, all you have to do is to go and find them, and then you will have them."

"But," said Al Hafed, "I don't know where to go."

"If you find a river that runs over white sands, between high mountains, in those white sands you will always find diamonds," answered the priest.

"But," asked Al Hafed, "do you believe there is such a river?"

"Plenty of them; all you have to do is just go where they are."

"Well," said Al Hafed, "I will go."

So he sold his farm, collected his money that was at interest, left his family in charge of a neighbor, and away he went in search of diamonds.

He began his search, very properly to my mind, at the Mountains of the Moon. Afterwards he came around into Palestine, and then wandered on into Europe. At last, when his money was all gone and he was in rags, poverty and wretchedness, he stood on the shore at Barcelona, in Spain, when a great tidal wave swept through the pillars of Hercules; and the poor, starving, afflicted stranger could not resist the awful temptation to cast himself into that incoming tide; and he sank beneath its foaming crest, never to rise in this life again.

When the old guide had told that story, he stopped the camel I was riding upon and went back to arrange the baggage on another camel, and I had an opportunity to muse over his story. And I asked myself this question: "Why did this old guide reserve this story for his *particular friends*?" But when he came back and took up the camel's halter once more, I found that this was the first story I ever heard wherein the hero was killed in the first chapter. For he went on into the second chapter, just as though there had been no break.

Said he: "The man who purchased Al Hafed's farm led his camel out into the garden to drink, and as the animal put his nose into the shallow waters of the garden brook, Al Hafed's successor noticed a curious flash of light from the white sands of the stream. Reaching in, he pulled out a black stone containing a strange eye of light. He took it into the house as a curious pebble and, putting it on the mantel that covered the central fire, went his way and forgot all about it.

"But not long after that that same old priest came to visit Al Hafed's successor. The moment he opened the door he noticed the flash of light. He rushed to the mantel and said: 'Here is a diamond! Here is a diamond! Has Al Hafed returned?'

"'Oh, no, Al Hafed has not returned and we have not heard from him since he went away, and that is not a diamond. It is nothing but a stone we found out in our garden.'

"'But,' said the priest, 'I know a diamond when I see it. I tell you that is a diamond.'

"Then together they rushed out into the garden. They stirred up the white sands with their fingers, and there came up other more beautiful, more valuable gems than the first.

"Thus," said the guide—and friends, it is historically true—"was discovered the diamond mines of Golconda, the most valuable diamond mines in the history of the ancient world."

Well, when the guide had added the second chapter to his story, he then took off his Turkish cap, and swung it in the air to call my special attention to the moral; those Arab guides always have morals to their stories, though the stories are not always moral.

He said to me, "Had Al Hafed remained at home, and dug in his own cellar, or underneath his own wheat field, instead of wretchedness, starvation, poverty and death in a strange land, he would have had ACRES OF DIAMONDS."

Acres of Diamonds! For every acre of that old farm, yes, every shovelful, afterwards revealed the gems which since have decorated the crowns of monarchs.

When the guide had added the moral to this story, I saw why he reserved it for his *particular friends*. But I didn't tell him that I could see it. It was that mean, old Arab's way of going around a thing, like a lawyer, and saying indirectly what he didn't dare say directly: that in his private opinion "there was a certain young man traveling down the Tigris River, who might better be at home, in America."

The complete text of Russell Conwell's "Acres of Diamonds" can be ordered by visiting, www.lifequestintl.com

Chapter 2
Diamonds Are a Girl's Best Friend

I love my wife. Shortly after I asked her to marry me, I suggested we go to a jeweler to pick out a diamond engagement ring (that should have been a clue right there that something was wrong with me—I asked her to marry me without a diamond in my pocket). "You don't have to do that," she said. "I don't want a diamond." I couldn't believe what I heard. "You don't want a diamond? I've never heard of a girl not wanting a diamond!" "Well, it's not that I don't want one— it's just that I know that you can't afford one big enough that I would want to wear," she responded. Wow! A realist and a pragmatist! And I could tell from the start that I would never have trouble finding out what she was thinking.

We did go to the jeweler—to buy a "moon stone," one of those big, translucent, oval-shaped, white stones. Let's just say it was an affordable option based on my available resources at the time. And my gold wedding band, which Pam purchased, cost more than her engagement ring.

For the next ten years, her comment about my inability to satisfy her taste in a diamond worked inside of me. As we started our tenth year of marriage together, I put together a plan to earn extra money by doing some moonlighting and I quietly set it aside until I had enough to go shopping. I found a modest one-half-carrot diamond (enough so you could see it, but not enough to impress the real diamond chasers) in a special antique setting and I prepared to surprise Pam on our tenth anniversary. We traveled to The Grand Hotel on Mackinac Island, location for the Christopher Reeve's movie *Somewhere in Time,* and spent three days on the island riding horses, sampling the famous Mackinac Island fudge, and rocking on what the resort claims as the longest front porch in the world. On the final night together, after dinner, I pulled out a small box, wrapped in gold foil and asked Pam if she would open it. It was the best surprise I ever gave her, and almost twenty years later I can still feel her response as she put this "respectable" ring on for the first time.

What makes diamonds so precious, so valued, and so extraordinary? They are unique gems, endowed with very special characteristics and uses. Industrial diamonds play a very important role in manufacturing because of their hardness and ability to cut every other material on earth, including steel. Industrial diamonds also dissipate heat very quickly. But, ultimately, the gem diamonds used in jewelry have no innate value—their value is determined entirely by those who take pleasure in purchasing and wearing them.

When I went shopping for Pam's diamond, I learned that a gem diamond is graded on its carat, clarity, color, and cut. The weight is measured by the carat, with one carat weighing two hundred milligrams. The clarity, or purity, of a gem is measured by the presence or absence of various kinds of flaws. These may include small foreign materials in the stone, and small bubbles or cracks that gemologists refer to as feathers. The color of most diamonds used in jewelry includes a faintly yellowish tint. A small percentage of diamonds is colorless, while a few possess a faint tinge of blue, red, brown, green, and even black. The cut of a gem diamond affects its value significantly, because a stone that is not properly cut at exactly the right angles does not show as much brilliance as one that is perfectly cut.

Cutting diamonds is a painstaking, messy, and noisy business. Highly trained workers, who take many years to learn to do their work skillfully, labor in unpleasant conditions and with little room for mistakes. The beauty of a diamond is caused, in large part, by the way it reflects light, bends rays of light, and breaks light up into all the colors of the rainbow. To produce the greatest possible brilliance, many little sides (facets) must be cut and polished at exactly the right angle.

A diamond's hardness, or toughness, is what makes it so valuable. This toughness is derived from the diamond's creation under extreme heat and pressure. The first diamonds were found in the sand and gravel of streambeds. Later, it was discovered that most diamonds are deep in the earth, in rock formations called pipes. These pipes are thought to be the throats of extinct volcanoes, and there are only four important diamond fields that have been found around the world—in Africa, India, Russia, and South America. Africa produces approximately seventy percent of the world's supply of diamonds, and Russia produces another twenty percent from the diamond fields of Siberia. Even in the most prodigious fields of the world, many tons of "blue" ground must be taken from deep in the earth just to obtain one small diamond.

The English word *diamond* is derived from the Greek word *adamao*, which means, "I subdue." A few years ago one of my sons spent several weeks in Tibet, where the word for *diamond* means "hidden potential."

So what relevance does all this information about diamonds have to our topic of hidden treasures? Are there some parallels that we can draw from what we know about diamonds that will help us as we go on our journey of finding the diamonds of mind, heart, body, and spirit within? What clues to searching for and mining inner treasures can you find in this allegory? Maybe taking a little time before you read on will help you think about your own hidden treasures in a different light as we begin our treasure hunt together.

Action Steps

1. Make a list of the attributes and uses of diamonds described in this chapter.

2. Next to each attribute define ways that it might be related to "diamonds" of the mind, heart, body, and spirit. (Example: diamonds are the result of heat and pressure—how might this attribute be related to the creation of treasures in the mind, heart, body or spirit?)

3. Write a paragraph about how diamonds are discovered,

prepared, and used, and how this could be useful in tapping your hidden treasures within.

Part I
Diamonds of the Mind

A group of children first visited a planetarium, then looked at a tiny flower. Afterward they drew on paper some of the things they had seen. One boy put a dot in the corner of the drawing. "This is me," he wrote, then added thoughtfully, "but I am bigger than the stars because I can think."

Chapter 3
"A Penny for Your Thoughts"

Has anyone ever offered you a "penny for your thoughts"? Such an offer usually comes when someone close to you notices a look in your eyes that indicates your mind is somewhere else, usually *way off* somewhere else.

Thoughts . . . have you ever wondered what role they play in our lives? Or where they come from? I have spent a lot of time thinking about thoughts and reading what others have to say about them.

For instance, the Bible says, "As a man thinks in his heart, so is he" (Proverbs 23:7). William James, a famous psychologist at the end of the 1800s, wrote a classic about this called, "As a Man Thinketh." Ralph Waldo Emerson wrote, "A man becomes what he thinks about all day long." Emerson also wrote, "Great men are they who see that spiritual is stronger than any material force, that thoughts rule the world."

Earl Nightingale, one of the American pioneers of personal development programs, recorded an album many years ago that produced the first and only gold record of a spoken presentation, "The Strangest Secret." He called this secret strange because it really doesn't have to be a secret at all—it is plain for everyone to see. The secret? A person becomes what he thinks about; therefore, we can change who we are and what we accomplish in life by changing what we think about.

So how important are your thoughts? And where do they come from? If what many different teachers of human behavior say is true, your thoughts are very important. Another way of asking this question is, "What are your thoughts worth?" It is obvious that some people's thoughts end up being worth a fortune! And, unfortunately, we also can see that some thoughts are worth little or nothing, resulting in pain and suffering in the lives of others because of what they cause a person to become.

So where do *your* thoughts come from? Do they come from a deliberate strategy to develop your fullest potential by interacting with people who represent what you hope to become? Do they come from meaningful reading and listening to inspirational audio or video tapes? Do they come from saturating your mind with the possibilities of what could happen with your life if you gave it your best effort? Do you exercise your "mental muscle" by memorizing significant quotes, your mission statement, and favorite statements of faith?

Or do your thoughts come from indiscriminate exposure to whatever ideas, images, and fantasies Hollywood, the tabloids, and office gossip bring your way? Do you allow your mind to be filled with scenes of violence, immoral behavior, abuse, and scandal? Do you expose your precious mental software to the criticalness, negativity, resentment, despair, and fear of those around you?

I've discovered that the right kind of thoughts don't come automatically in my life. I have to work at them. There are several ways I do this. I try to spend time every day praying, reading from the Bible and other inspirational books, and journaling as a discipline to control my attitude and thoughts. I listen to CDs. I focus my mind and imagination on my life mission and goals, approaching problems with a positive, can-do attitude. I try to remember to always express gratitude toward others. One of my favorite verses from the Bible comes from Philippians 4:8, which says, "Finally, brothers, whatever is true, whatever is noble, whatever is right, whatever is pure, whatever is lovely, whatever is admirable—if anything is excellent or praiseworthy—think about such things."

Legendary golfer Arnold Palmer has a single plaque hanging on a wall in his office. The plaque reveals why he has been successful on and off the golf course. It reads:

If you *think* you are beaten, you are.
If you *think* you dare not, you don't.
If you like to win but *think* you can't,
It's almost certain that you won't.

Life's battles don't always go
To the stronger woman or man,
But sooner or later, those who win
Are those who *think* they can.

Another writer from another time captured the idea of the power in our thoughts. His name was Samuel Smiles, and he wrote about this cerebral power in his book, *Life and Labor*, which was published in 1887. I have changed what he wrote just a little to tell the story of the power in our thoughts. It goes like this: "Sow a thought, and you will reap an attitude. Sow an attitude, and you will reap an act. Sow an act, and you will reap a habit. Sow a habit, and you will reap a character. And sow a character, and you will reap a destiny."

The power of your thoughts—maybe one of the greatest powers you have today. And definitely worth a lot more than a penny!

Action Steps

1. Pretend that thoughts are magic, that whatever you think, whether good or bad, will instantly appear. Write out ten things you would think about if they could happen instantly.

2. What if thoughts really are magic and they really will materialize . . . if only you can hold on to them long enough? How can you anchor your thoughts in your mind so that they will move you toward your desired destiny day after day until their fulfillment? Make a list of three things you can do to anchor these thoughts in your mind.

3. Set aside fifteen minutes every day for the next week to review your top ten list of thoughts and to refine them until they capture your commitment to pursue them to fulfillment.

Chapter 4
Unlimited Possibilities

"The undeveloped piece of property with the greatest
potential is still between the ears."
— Anonymous

Do you ever wish you had more of something? Could you
fulfill a dream if you had more money? Would you take on a
new project that could significantly change your life if you
had more time? What more would you attempt to do if you
could tap into more energy?

Each of us has a limited amount of these resources (money,
time, energy) that provide the opportunities for improving our
lives. But we all have some. Some of us have extra time. What
other explanation can there be for the huge number of hours
that are spent in front of the television each year? Some of us
have extra energy. Just look at the explosion of the leisure
industry over the past twenty years. (I have discovered that
there is a great difference between "leisure" and "rest"!) And,
believe it or not, some of us have so much money that we don't
know what to do with it all. How else can we explain the
rampant consumerism that exists in our world today, forever
promising happiness but mostly delivering layer after layer
of complexity and distraction from true personal fulfillment?
Though the vast majority of people living in developed nations
have an abundance of these resources, it appears we lack the
wisdom to recognize how to use them to uncover and pursue
our greatest potential.

I am awestruck by the opportunities that are available to us
compared with the generations that preceded us. Never before
have there been as many new resources to improve the quality
and productivity of our lives. Several years ago I heard a
speaker point out that the modern conveniences we enjoy in
our homes represent the equivalent of approximately two
hundred personal servants in ancient times. He made this

proclamation before the advent of home computers, the Internet, e-mail, cell phones, online banking, and many other technologies that have connected us to an ever-expanding world of convenience and efficiency. How many "servants" do we have working on our behalf today?

Never before have there been as many millionaires on the face of the earth as there are today. Never before have there been as many diversions for our time, and never before have there been as many ways to increase—and spend—our energy. Never before have there been as many charitable organizations doing as much humanitarian work. Most important, never before has our understanding of human potential and the path to achievement been as comprehensive as it is today.

Have you ever taken time to think deeply about your personal potential? The word *potential* means the latent, unrealized power to become what has not yet come into being. How does this concept of potential affect you? How important is it in your life? What is your absolute greatest potential? What are you consciously, deliberately doing to move toward the fulfillment of this potential? What great thing would you attempt to do if you knew you could not fail?

H. G. Wells, the famous novelist and historian, said that wealth, notoriety, place, and power are no measures of success whatever. The only true measure of success is the ratio between what we might have been and what we have become. What is the ratio between what you might have been and what you have become? What unrealized potential still resides within, waiting to be brought forth?

A writer asked George Bernard Shaw to play the "what if" game shortly before he died. He said, "Mr. Shaw, you have visited with some of the most famous people in the world. You have known royalty, world-renowned authors, artists, teachers, and dignitaries from every part of the world. If you could live your life over and be anybody you have known, or any person from history, who would you choose to be?"

Shaw replied, "I would choose to be the man George Bernard Shaw could have been, but never was."

Pursuing your potential is not found in attempting to be like someone else, or achieving what someone else has achieved. It is a pursuit of the untapped reservoirs of potential within yourself. And few people come anywhere close to exhausting the resources within. John Maxwell, author of *The 21 Irrefutable Laws of Leadership*, wrote, "Many intelligent adults are restrained in thoughts, actions and results. They never move further than the boundaries of their self-imposed limitation."

One of the greatest demonstrations of pursuing personal potential is the story of Helen Keller. She lost her sight and hearing in 1882, through illness, when she was only nineteen months old. She became a wild, rebellious, uncontrolled youngster until a nearly blind teacher was attracted to the challenge of teaching her. As a result of Anne Sullivan Macy's belief in Helen's potential, she later attended Radcliffe College, studying French and Greek and typing her papers using a Braille-keyed typewriter. She went on to become a world-famous prodigy, raising funds for the American Foundation for the Blind, lobbying for change around the world, and brightening the spirits of wounded soldiers during World War II.

Although she lived in a world of silence and darkness, Helen Keller refused to let a disability stand in the way of her potential. She altered people's views of individuals with disabilities, while expanding the awareness of their own potential. Her greatest capacities were tapped because she never made peace with the status quo and she never tried to be like anyone else. Instead, she invested all of her efforts toward becoming the best that she could be. She saw herself as a change agent, having discovered the possibilities for positive change through her inner journey of self-awareness and achievement. Mark Twain said of her, "She will be as famous a thousand years from now as she is today."

What about you? What is your untapped potential? How can

you convert your view of life from "what is" to "what can be"? Winners do not leave the development of their potential to chance. They pursue it systematically with the excitement of knowing there are unlimited possibilities residing within, waiting to be discovered and put to work.

Actions Steps

1. Set aside one hour in the next few days to explore your potential. Write across the top of a page, "What is my true potential in life?" Then jot down whatever answers come into your mind.

- Journal about what kind of person you could become if you pursued it with focus and discipline. This is your character potential.

- Journal about the greatest goals you can imagine achieving. This helps to define your achievement potential.

- Journal about your greatest dreams for prosperity and abundance. This will help define your reward potential.

2. Make a list of what other people have told you about your potential (what you do well, what they recognize as unique talent, and so on). What can you learn about your future potential by contemplating this list?

3. What childhood dreams about your future did you have? Have you achieved them? Are you still pursuing them?

Points to Ponder

"Few men during their lifetime come anywhere near exhausting the resources within them. There are deep wells of strength that are seldom used." — Richard E. Boyd, author

"I have no doubt whatever that most people live, whether physically, intellectually, or morally, in a very restricted circle of their potential being . . . we all have reservoirs of life to draw upon of which we do not dream." — William James, psychologist

UNLIMITED POSSIBILITIES

Chapter 5
Reading for Diamonds

"You are the same today as you'll be in five years except for
the people you meet and the books you read."
— Charles "Tremendous" Jones, author of *Life Is Tremendous*

I have been privileged to meet and learn from many great
people throughout my lifetime. Some of them are family
members who influenced me at key times when decisions I
made were critical to my future. Some of them have been close
friends who had just the right word of encouragement when I
needed it. Some had a word of caution, even rebuke, when I
needed a course correction. But many of the people who have
made the greatest difference in my life have never met me.
They don't have the slightest idea about how much they have
changed my life. That said, I am sure I have met them and I
know many of them better than my neighbor. How is this
possible? Because some of the people who have had the greatest
influence in my life are the ones I have met in books.

Books are indispensable for discovering the diamonds of your
mind. I think they are more important than any other form of
communication we receive today. Do you know why? In an
audio or video presentation, through television or the cinema,
you hear and see the speakers or performers and they add
their inflections, expressions, and personalities to the
presentation. But when you read a book, you become a partner
with the author. The author provides the words and the rest is
up to you. You read a book in your own voice, with your own
inflections and nuances of awareness. This can be very
exciting—how many times have you heard someone say, "The
book was much better than the movie"?

In a book you become a party to the story, albeit usually a
third-party observer. You identify intimately with the cast of
characters, you wrestle with the conflict, your emotions are
engaged in the dramatic tension, and you eagerly read on to

the appropriate resolution. It is the closest thing to experiencing the event yourself. Actually, you are experiencing the event—in your imagination!

The main thing that inspires me to keep reading is a desire to grow and change. Whether it is reading a book on personal development, health, or organizational management, a captivating novel, or the Bible, I'm motivated by the way books change my outlook on life. It's a shame that most adults don't take advantage of the opportunities available to them in books; approximately sixty percent of all adults never read a nonfiction book after graduating from school!

Many years ago I decided that I would spend a minimum of fifteen minutes a day reading from a book. I have not been perfect in fulfilling this commitment. I have wandered away from it over the years, only to recommit myself when I recognized that I was missing the stimulation books cause in my thinking. Even with my lapses of discipline, I have managed to read hundreds, if not thousands, of books during my adult life. It is impossible to measure the impact this reading has had on my life.

I discovered it doesn't matter how much I read, just that I keep reading. And I believe that almost anyone, reading just thirty minutes a day, can read ten to twelve books a year. The accumulated impact of reading good books over many years is such that you will never fully realize the great favor you are doing for yourself when you read.

Books provide food for your mind. They feed your understanding, increase your mental strength, inspire commitment, and refresh your perspective. J. C. Penney, the founder of the department store by the same name, stated,

> The reading of good books is one of the most
> helpful ways in which young people can develop
> themselves. To read good books casually will not
> suffice. One must study every sentence and make
> sure of its full message. Good writers do not

intend that we should get their full meaning without effort. They expect us to dig as one is compelled to dig for gold. Gold, you know, is not generally found in large openings, but in tiny veins. The ore must be subjected to a white heat in order to get the pure gold. Remember this when you read.

Young men and women who are seeking to learn all they can, have minds capable of receiving and retaining new impressions. There is nothing that will strengthen the mind, broaden the vision, enrich the soul more than the reading of good books.

If someone asked you for a list of the ten most important books in your life, could you produce it? How did these books change your life? Do you have a list of good books you are preparing to read now? Do you keep a list of books recommended by others? Remember, "You are the same today as you will be in five years except for the people you meet and the books you read."

Action Steps

1. Make a list of the most influential books you have read and write a paragraph explaining why this book was important to you.

2. Make a list of ten books you would like to read during the next twelve months to enrich your life.

3. Reserve thirty minutes a day for the next month to read a book that will challenge you to grow. Read it slowly, thinking as much or more than reading, and take notes about what is stirred in your mind through reading.

Points to Ponder

"How many a man has dated a new era in his life from the reading of a book?" — Henry David Thoreau

"The book to read is not the one which thinks for you, but the one which makes you think. No book in the world equals the Bible for that." — James McCosh, philosopher

"I cannot live without books." — Thomas Jefferson

"Without books, God is silent, justice dormant, natural science at a stand, philosophy lame, letters dumb, and all things involved in darkness." — Bartholini, Danish physician

"Books are those faithful mirrors that reflect to our mind the minds of sages and heroes." — Edward Gibbon, English historian

"The books we read should be chosen with great care, that they may be, as an Egyptian king wrote over his library, 'The medicines of the soul.' Be as careful of the books you read, as of the company you keep; for your habits and character will be as much influenced by the former as by the latter." — Paxton Hood, English clergyman

Chapter 6
The Greatest Hidden Treasure

Driving from Chicago to Detroit one afternoon in 1986, I felt a bolt of inspiration from heaven about one of the greatest, most powerful secrets of the human journey. As I communed with God that sunny afternoon, I discovered the greatest of all hidden treasures. For the first time, I saw it clearly and recognized it so intimately that I could reach out and touch it. It's as if I was lifting up the cover of an old treasure chest and looking inside at one of the most brilliant collections of jewels and precious stones the world had ever seen, and there in the middle was one of the rarest gems of all.

It is a hidden treasure so powerful that once you discover it, you will have in your possession a map so clear, so defining, so powerful that you will never go another day for the rest of your life without finding profound opportunity in that day. It is a treasure that is available to every living person, regardless of their education, their past failures or successes, their oppressions, or their limitations. I can't give this gem to you, but I can show you where it is and help you understand how to uncover it so that things will never be the same.

Do you want it? You see, if you don't really want it, it doesn't do me any good to point you toward it, because you will leave empty-handed unless you want it. It is one of the strangest secrets of mankind—strange because it is so obvious, but secret because even though it is obvious to those who have discovered it, it remains invisible to those who have yet to understand its power. And the first step to understanding its power is to want it.

Second, you must be willing to bow down in humility to receive it. Just as if it was buried in the sand and required that you get down on your knees and dig with your hands to uncover it, you must be teachable and humble to receive the illumination, the revelation of this hidden treasure. You see, without the childlike attitude of teachableness and humility, you may scorn or ridicule this treasure and never discover the true brilliance and luster of the gem you are about to uncover. Thousands of people have found this treasure throughout history, but only when they set aside their cynicism and unbelief and allowed themselves to believe once again in the miracle, the mystery of a hidden treasure. Can you bow down in humility and receive it with the faith of a child?

Third, you must protect it once you have found it. It is a strange kind of gem, because its final value is determined by how much value you place in it. To some it is a small, barely noteworthy trinket of costume jewelry. For others, it revolutionizes their lives and causes them to rise to levels of success and achievement beyond their wildest dreams. To those who totally employ this treasure and use it to its fullest potential, there is the likelihood of sharing riches and jewels with thousands of others. Many of those who protected this treasure and honored it as sacred ended up being written about in history books, becoming known to generation after generation because they learned how to embrace as sacred what you are about to discover for yourself.

This gem that is so precious, yet so seldom uncovered and polished to reflect its true value, blinded me when I discovered it, forcing me to pull off the road in a moment of sacred communion as I came face-to-face with possibly the greatest human treasure of all—the power to choose.

Like no other time before, I saw it crystal clear: I have been given the power to choose. I don't have the power to change everything around me, but I have the power to choose how I respond to everything around me. I don't have the power to change people, but I have the power to change how I respond to people. I don't have the power to change the laws of nature, but I have the power to choose how I employ the laws of nature.

I have the power to choose good over evil, no matter how much evil is around me. I have the power to choose love and compassion instead of criticism and resentment, no matter how much criticism and resentment is around me. I have the power to choose perseverance, even if everyone else around me quits. I have the power to choose health, even if others choose disease. I have the power to choose gratitude, even if everyone else is complaining.

I have the power to choose! I can choose optimism instead of pessimism. I can choose love, joy, peace, patience, kindness, goodness, faithfulness, gentleness, and self-control (see Galatians 5:22–23).

That day I clearly understood, with a divinely inspired clarity, that my future does not depend on those around me, the economy, chance, or fate—because I have been given the power to choose.

Of course, this power is not mine alone. Since then I have seen this power working in countless others who have found the same hidden treasure. I remember reading about a Jewish man named Viktor Frankel, who wrote the book *Man's Search for Meaning*. He told about his years in a death camp during World War II. He discovered that the prison guards could torture him, deny him sunlight, water, and food, curse him, and even kill him. But one thing they couldn't do was take away his power to choose what went on inside his head while they were doing all this. So while they tortured him, he would picture himself in a beautiful, soothing place surrounded by his loved ones with every pleasure at his beck and call.

Then I think of Bob Wieland, who had both legs blown off from a grenade that landed on him in Vietnam. But instead of wallowing in self-pity and defeat, Bob exercised his power to choose—and that power resulted in him setting a world record in the bench press, becoming the strength training coach for the Green Bay Packers, and running the entire twenty-six-mile Marine marathon in Washington, D.C., *on his hands*, all because he discovered the power to choose.

What a powerful hidden treasure I had discovered! But it was also more than a little scary. If I truly had this power at my disposal, what should I choose? On that drive around Lake Michigan I was startled to realize that with power comes the responsibility to use that power for good. For I was suddenly aware that we have the power to choose our actions, but none of us has the power to choose the consequences of those actions.

Over the years a number of people have let me down: they abandoned me, they criticized me, they ignored me, and some attacked me, but I still have the power to choose. There have been economic hardships through the years. At one point several years ago, I lost eighty percent of my income overnight and we had to sell our house quickly to avoid bankruptcy; but even then we had the power to choose how we would respond and what we would do next. More recently a career change, some poor investments, and a new business start-up drained almost all the resources we spent the last twenty-five years building, once again giving us the opportunity to choose our response to times of challenge and change.

Probably most discouraging have been the times I let myself down, not living up to the standards of excellence and dedication that I want for myself, for my family, and my work. But even stacked up against the deep disappointment of my own failures, I still have the power to choose.

Who knows what the future will bring? Who knows what new challenges we will face, what new trials we will endure, what suffering and hardship we must still overcome? Regardless of what will come our way, one of the greatest endowments we have during our journey on earth is the power to choose. How are you using this power in your life today?

Have you discovered this hidden treasure within? It is your greatest resource. It holds all the promise for your future, regardless of your age or previous experiences. It cries out within you, calling for your faith, calling for your hope, calling you to action.

The greatest treasure you can have is already within you. Open up the chest and look upon your hidden treasure—you, my friend, have the power to choose.

Action Steps

1. Make a list of the five most important decisions you have made in your life and how your choices changed your destiny.

2. Think about someone close to you who chose to go against the current and how this choice shaped his or her life.

3. What choices do you face right now? How can you employ your power to choose a new, higher course in your life that will create something beautiful, strong, and enduring? Take time to journal about choices you can make that will give deep meaning to your life.

Points to Ponder

"We can choose our thoughts, attitudes, and actions, but we cannot choose the consequences of our thoughts, attitudes, and actions, because whatever we sow will be multiplied back to us." — Price family proverb

"It is not in life's chances but in its choices that happiness comes to the heart of the individual."— Anonymous

"We are free up to the point of choice, then the choice controls the chooser." — Mary Crowley, American author

"The Road Not Taken"
Two roads diverged in a yellow wood,
And sorry I could not travel both
And be one traveler, long I stood
And looked down one as far as I could
To where it bent in the undergrowth;

Then took the other, as just as fair,

And having perhaps the better claim,
Because it was grassy and wanted wear;
Though as for that the passing there
Had worn them really about the same,

And both that morning equally lay
In leaves no step had trodden black.
Oh, I kept the first for another day!
Yet knowing how way leads on to way,
I doubted if I should ever come back.

I shall be telling this with a sigh
Somewhere ages and ages hence:
Two roads diverged in a wood, and I—
I took the one less traveled by,
And that has made all the difference.
— Robert Frost

Chapter 7
Remembering Forward

"Vision . . . the art of seeing things invisible." That is how Jonathan Swift described vision back in 1726 in his essay, "Thoughts on Various Subjects." Peter Koestenbaum, another philosopher, wrote, "Vision is not necessarily having a plan, but having a mind that always plans. In sum, vision means to be in touch with the unlimited potential and expanse of this marvelous instrument called the human mind." Helen Keller said, "The most pathetic person in the world is someone who has sight but has no vision!"

Vision seems to be an elusive, yet important, life principle. Your vision describes the ideal future for you to attain. It provides meaning and direction while rousing you to break through present limitations. Vision uses the same mental capacities as memory. Memory is a vivid mental picture of the past. In a sense, vision is "remembering forward" by creating a vivid mental picture of the future. Holding a vivid picture in your mind of your desired future will unleash your creative efforts and breed the desire and energy necessary to perform.

Most people shy away from trying to develop a clear, dynamic vision of the future. There are many reasons for this reticence. For some, it is too scary to think about taking an active role in shaping their future. They would rather just let things happen. Many people lack the confidence that anything can change from the way it has always been. They have limited themselves by past failures and disappointments. Others are content to move along with the rest of the crowd as if they were part of a herd of animals, never breaking away to express their unique talents or pursue their dreams. Last of all, some people think they would be offending God, or somehow violating a relationship of submission and obedience by developing a vision that includes "the desires of their heart."

Yet a study of every great leader or achiever in history reveals the importance of vision. Vision is neither moral nor immoral. It is simply a vehicle we use to express and pursue a better future. Effective vision is empowered by strong desire and inner drive that won't rest until it is fulfilled. This kind of vision is one of the fundamental traits shared in common by anyone who has ever accomplished great things. When Martin Luther King Jr. stood on the steps of the Lincoln Memorial on August 28, 1963, he proclaimed four words that have been heard around the world. "I have a dream . . ." was his description of a vision. The power of vision caused him to rise above racism and many other obstacles to become a leader and source of inspiration for millions around the world. The words of his speech on that day in 1963 continue to ring out again and again, encouraging us to look to the future with hope and expectation that new achievements and new opportunities are waiting for our commitment to bring them into reality.

The creation of vision is fueled by desire, either as a result of some deficit in our lives or because of a compelling opportunity. All human beings experience desire, or need, in four basic areas. First, we all have physical needs that we naturally seek to satisfy. These include food, clothing, shelter, and safety. In our modern society, leisure and recreation also have become physical desires that many pursue. After our physical needs are met, we begin to pursue the fulfillment of social needs. These include meaningful relationships that are filled with love, appreciation, loyalty, and fellowship. In addition, we each have a natural desire to improve ourselves in a variety of different ways. These include, but are not limited to, intellectual, artistic, and athletic pursuits. Last of all, each of us has a deeper need to make a contribution, to make a difference in the lives of those around us.

There are several disciplines you can employ to enlarge your vision. Here are some that have worked for me.

First, read. There is so much wisdom, inspiration, and vision available through books. Biographies are particularly beneficial because they show how ordinary people often produce extraordinary results. It isn't important how much you read, just that you keep reading fifteen to thirty minutes every day. This is food for your mind. A well-nourished mind will spawn vision!

Second, pursue recorded stories of other people's lives. Through audio and video programs you can expose yourself to the ideas and experiences of ordinary people made great through great vision. Stir your imagination by watching a movie about the life of Gandhi or witnessing the transformation of Oskar Schindler in *Schindler's List*. Awaken your capacity for believing in great possibilities by listening to Earl Nightingale, or discover the joy of redesigning your life by listening to Cheryl Richardson. We have more access to inspiring stories than at any other time in history. Exposing ourselves to these stories can unleash a deep spring of creativity as we shape our vision for the future.

Third, expand your vision by keeping a journal. Writing out your thoughts, desires, needs, and dreams is an invigorating exercise. If you make journaling a regular discipline, you will find moments of intense inspiration that expand your vision beyond anything you have ever dreamed possible. Journaling helps you focus your thoughts and crystallize the ideas that can become the core of a captivating vision for your future.

The fourth discipline that has helped me to expand my vision is meditation. In this instance, I'm not referring to the Eastern practice of emptying your mind. Instead, this is taking time to set aside all the urgent, daily distractions so you can consider what possibilities your future might hold. It means to wrestle through what is most important in your life, what kind of person you want to become, and what great things you would attempt if you knew you could not fail.

However you get it, vision is vital to reaching your fullest potential. No matter what your age or place in life, the power of your vision will become the reality of your future. One of my mentors on this subject has been Napoleon Hill, the author of *Think & Grow Rich*, who wrote, "Whatever you can vividly imagine, ardently desire, sincerely believe and enthusiastically act upon, must inevitably come to pass."

I have spent twenty years contemplating, testing, and sharing this simple quote with others. I'm more convinced today than ever that this statement is absolutely true in its reliability. It contains the essence of our human journey, complete with all of the safeguards necessary to stand the test of time. Each segment of this quote is worthy of discussion. However, none of it is useful without vision. In Hill's words, vision is defined as "whatever you can vividly imagine." Every human achievement must first pass through the elucidation of vision before it has any chance of becoming a reality. (Some of my spiritual friends are fearful of the creative power of vision and they prefer to walk in God's vision rather than take responsibility for their own. But I'm convinced the power and mandate to develop vision is, in itself, one of the greatest gifts we receive from God.)

How would you develop vision if you knew you could not fail? If we assume that your future is yours to create, how would you go about shaping your vision of a future reality? It waits for your careful consideration and response! Unfortunately, we often fail to define our dreams for the future because of fear or a feeling of inadequacy. We prefer to trust ourselves to "fate" and end up surrendering to the circumstances that surround us. Occasionally, we take the first step of identifying our vision only to be derailed by the onslaught of urgent activities in our lives that cause us to lose the focus of what we want to become and to accomplish over a longer period of time.

I must admit that I have lost this focus many times throughout my life. However, even with my inconsistencies, the limited clarity of vision I have experienced has provided excitement and purpose to my life. Goals and desires that I thought would take a lifetime to accomplish have unfolded in a small portion of the time I expected. As I have accepted the power and opportunity inherent in "vividly imagining," I have watched change take place in me and in my circumstances far faster and greater than I thought possible. And the same can happen for you.

How do you want your life to change? Will you move to a new home, or take on a new job? Do you long to fulfill a secret dream of significance? What great contributions do you want to make to society, based on your unique talents and motivations? Where will you travel? How do you want to affect other people's lives? How specific and detailed can you paint this picture? Try to imagine as much detail as possible. How deep and strong is your desire for this vision? What sacrifices are you willing to make for the fulfillment of your dream?

Finally, what kind of activities do you need to fill your life with to fulfill your vision? Are there others who have already walked the path you seek? How did they do it? Are they available for mentoring you as you take new steps of faith? What new skills or knowledge will you need to acquire? Most of all, what benefits will you enjoy as a result of fulfilling your dreams?

The unfortunate reality is that most people will not take this challenge seriously. They will either discount these suggestions as irrelevant to their struggles in life, or they will decide it is too much work to create a clear vision for the future. Or, some will agree this might make a difference in their lives. However, they will quickly become distracted by their long list of urgent tasks or a busy schedule, never taking the time to seize the higher ground that a well-defined vision can provide.

How about you? Will you recognize the treasures waiting for you if you create and pursue a great vision? If so, you are about to enter into the greatest years of your life, with rewards beyond your present ability to imagine. Regardless of your age, wealth, education, or social standing, you can begin to create a new, exciting chapter in your life by "remembering forward."

Action Steps

1. Make a list of your top ten heroes, either still living or from

history. What attributes or achievements do you admire in them? What if these same attributes or achievements could be realized through you?

2. Pretend you are attending your ninetieth birthday party and your closest friends and family are each speaking to honor you. Pick five of them (family members, friends, coworkers, service club associates, and one who observed you from a distance) and write out what they would say about you if you achieved your highest aspirations.

3. Write out the bravest, most exciting, and rewarding vision of the next ten years of your life as you can imagine. Make this description as vivid and detailed as possible, realizing that the more specific you capture this vision, the greater impact it will have on your future journey.

Points to Ponder

"Whatever you can vividly imagine, ardently desire, sincerely believe and enthusiastically act upon, must inevitably come to pass." — Napoleon Hill

"If you don't know where you are going, you may end up somewhere else." — Yogi Berra

"The world of tomorrow belongs to the people who have the vision of today." — Rev. Robert Schuller

Chapter 8
Making Sense of Goals

The beginning of "diamond hunting" is belief. Unless you believe there are gems present, the work of uncovering them is too hard, too long, and too speculative. I may tell you to go out into your backyard and start digging for diamonds and you may believe me for a day, maybe a week, maybe even a month. But unless you understand something about the science of geology and recognize the conditions under which diamonds exist, you will begin to question my advice and quit your quest for diamonds long before any successful discovery occurs.

And so it is with diamonds of the mind. Until you begin to recognize the power of your thoughts and how they can change your life, it just looks like a common backyard within. It doesn't matter what thoughts you have or how you seek to control them—it is just another "backyard." Until you are undone by the revelation of the infinite potential that resides within you, you cannot possibly put in the hard work necessary to do something beyond what you previously thought was possible. Until you are persuaded through reading and listening to the testimonies of others that there is a higher, more joyful existence than comfort and convenience, you will be content in only chasing appetites and passions. Either you will be content maintaining your present circumstance, or at best, you will be satisfied seeking for just a little more. (I remember hearing someone describe prosperity as making $15,000 more than you are currently making.) Until you realize that an immeasurable potential for treasures will remain dormant within you apart from developing your power of choice and creating a compelling vision for you life, all you will see is a backyard full of dirt. For a variety of reasons, you will probably do some landscaping and clean up the outward appearance of your yard. But without thinking, imagining, contemplating, and dreaming, you will never discover your hidden treasures.

Remember Al Hafed in our opening story, "Acres of Diamonds"? The storyteller told us that he was "wealthy because he was contented and contented because he was wealthy"—until the priest told him all about diamonds. Once he learned what diamonds were and how they could change his life, we read that "Al Hafed went to bed a poor man. He wanted a whole mine of diamonds."

Hopefully, you are experiencing two essential emotions as we share this book together. First, my prayer is that you have captured a glimpse of your infinite potential and the great opportunity you have to blossom into someone beyond your current capacity to comprehend. Perhaps you have been sparked with an excitement that has interrupted the normal routines of your day and caused you, even if only for brief moments, to experience the first young shoots of belief in some great, overwhelming dream for your future. This is the first essential response in the quest for hidden treasures. Second, you also should feel fear and apprehension concerning this quest; that if you really pursue your emerging vision you will be made the fool and will squander what little you already have. The combination of these two emotions is one of the clearest indicators that hidden treasures exist and they are within your grasp.

How do we transition from the world of visions, dreams, and hopes within to the world of the "second creation" that makes these thoughts a reality? What bridge can we cross that turns these electromagnetic impulses into authentic certainties? This bridge between what you presently are and what you will become is the bridge of goals.

Goals provide the "cutting and polishing" of your hidden treasures. They take the raw material and put it to use in a productive manner, improving and enlarging your life in the world around you. To use another analogy, goals harness the innate power within, much the same way that a hydroelectric plant can turn running water into enough electrical force to light up a city. Yet for some reason, this bridge of goals has never been properly built or utilized in most people's lives.

A famous study from Yale University helps to illustrate this point. Social scientists began this study in 1953 by interviewing the entire graduating class of Yale, asking a wide variety of questions. One of the more profound questions was, "Do you have a set of written goals for your life?" They discovered that three percent of the graduating class had a set of written goals for their lives and the remaining ninety-seven percent were waiting to discover what opportunities their circumstances might present. Twenty years later, in 1973, they resurveyed the remaining survivors of the class of '53—and they found out that the three percent with written goals had accumulated more financial net worth than the other ninety-seven percent combined! Imagine that! The three percent with written goals had more accumulated net worth than the other ninety-seven percent combined, who were allowing circumstances to dictate their plans. Though I have reported this study to literally thousands of people over the past twenty years, I would have to estimate that it has had little or no impact on approximately ninety-seven percent of the people with whom I have shared.

A more recent study is equally impressive. A group of regular goal setters in New York was studied to determine the impact of having written goals in their lives. The conclusion, which speaks volumes about the power of setting goals, was simple and dramatic: People who write their goals down, on average, achieve ninety-seven percent of all the goals they write down. What greater inspiration do we need to grab a piece of paper and start recording what we hope to become, accomplish, or have?

In light of the significant benefits of creating, writing, and pursuing goals, why don't we do it? I am aware of at least three reasons. First, most of us have given up on goals because we tried to write some in the past, only to be disappointed when the "goal fairy" didn't show up to deliver the promised magic that made our goals painlessly come into reality. As a result, we have become cynical about the practice of goal setting and opt for the path of least resistance, trying to make the most of the circumstances we are in. Second, most of us have never been taught how to write smart goals. We can write down what we want to have happen, but we don't know how to create a step-by-step blueprint that yields the end result we want. Third, many of us have never recognized that a goal is *not* the true source of power for change. It is simply the mechanism through which the inner power flows to facilitate change (the hydroelectric plant is worthless without the flow of water). The true sources of change are vision and choice; goals are simply the power plant through which these treasures travel to capture and direct the power within. If we haven't developed a compelling vision and recognized the power of personal choice, our goals are empty turbines that are doomed to quit turning for lack of water flowing down the stream.

Powerful goals are not the vision; they are vehicles to pursue the vision. They contain and define our vision with a laser focus to bring about significant change in our lives. Many speakers on goal setting have defined them as SMART goals, meaning they are:

Specific – written down in specific language so there is no question about what we seek to accomplish.
Measurable – clear quantification of what will be accomplished so there is no question when we have crossed the finish line.
Achievable – they are within our power and abilities to accomplish.
Realistic – given our current set of circumstances, we can complete the tasks necessary to bring a goal to fruition (in this way goals are very different from vision, which is often unrealistic at the time we first embrace it).
Time-bound – deadlines for various milestones along the way as well as the final completion date.

Once you have written SMART goals, try the following ways to anchor them in your field of vision:

1. List as many benefits as you can think of for achieving each goal. Referring to this list when you are "climbing the hill" can strengthen your resolve to finish the climb in the midst of weariness, discouragement, and doubt.

2. Identify all of the obstacles you may run into during the pursuit of your goal and create a strategy for turning these stumbling blocks into stepping stones along the way. One way I develop an appreciation for obstacles is by viewing them as soldiers put in the path to keep others from getting to my treasures before me.

3. Identify the new skills and knowledge you will need to develop in order to achieve your goal. A visionary goal will always require change and growth in you as an individual.

4. List the people or groups from whom you will need assistance to achieve your goal.

5. Create an accountability list of behaviors you will need to practice on a daily and weekly basis to achieve your goal. These are specific tasks that need to be completed—and often repeated—on a daily or weekly basis in order to move in the direction of your goal completion.

6. Create a visual representation of your goal, either in pictures or words, to keep in front of you every day so you don't lose sight of your focus. I place a printed copy of my goal on my car visor and read it out loud every time I get out of my car to drive it deep into my subconscious.

7. Make a goal a nonnegotiable priority in your life that comes before comfort or convenience—in other words, no pleasure or leisure activities until after you have completed the daily tasks that relate to goal completion.

Years ago, advertising legend David Ogilvy set out to establish a great advertising agency within a dozen years. At the time he was a small tobacco farmer in Pennsylvania. On his second day of business he made a list of five clients he most wanted to get. They were Bristol-Myers, Lever Brothers, Shell Oil Company, General Foods, and Campbell Soup Company. Eventually, he had them all.

When you have created an ambitious vision and immersed

yourself in the revelation of your hidden treasures, SMART goals will provide you with the focus and game plan to make the impossible come true—at least ninety-seven percent of the time! Are those odds worth betting on?

Action Steps

1. Referring to the journaling you did for your ten-year vision, pick one particular part of that vision and create one SMART goal that will move you toward the fulfillment of your vision.

2. After creating one SMART goal, make a list of the benefits, obstacles, new skills, people who can assist you, and behaviors necessary to achieve your goal.

3. Create a visual representation of this one goal (either pictorial or verbal) and put this in a prominent place where you will review this goal every day. Make a nonnegotiable agreement with yourself to pursue this goal as your top priority until it is completed.

This exercise is designed for the completion of *one goal only*. Until you have developed the ability to focus on and achieve one goal, it is a mistake to commit to several. Start slow and make sure you succeed. As you develop your goal-achieving "muscles," you will increase your capacity to manage several goals at once. However, start with one and add another only after you have completed the first.

For advanced instruction on goal setting, visit our Web site at www.lifequestintl.com.

Points to Ponder

"Before you can score, you must first have a goal." — Anonymous

"The future does not get better by hope, it gets better by plan.

And to plan for the future we need goals." — Jim Rohn, motivational speaker

"It must be born in mind that the tragedy of life doesn't lie in not reaching your goal. The tragedy lies in having no goal to reach. It isn't calamity to die with dreams unfulfilled, but it is a calamity to not dream. It is not a disgrace not to reach the stars, but it is a disgrace to have no stars to reach for. Not failure, but low aim is sin." — Helmut Schmidt, former West German chancellor

"Obstacles are those frightful things you see when you take your eyes off the goal." — Hannah More, American author

Chapter 9
Enlisting Providence

"A dedication to a long-term course of action; involvement; engagement." That's how *Webster's New World Dictionary* defines *commitment*. What does this word mean to you? What role does commitment play in your life? And how much power comes from the commitments you make?

Many psychologists believe that our inner capacity and self-esteem are directly related to our commitments. They observe that people who make and keep commitments to themselves consistently have more self-confidence than those who live in the arena of wishful thinking, or who leave a long trail of broken promises.

Psychologists postulate further that if you want to increase your level of confidence and self-esteem, it always begins with making and keeping commitments to yourself. Because of this, they recommend creating *short-term* goals that you have a ninety percent chance of achieving. Though these goals may not seem very demanding, each fulfilled goal adds a new thread into the fabric of your self-confidence and increases your ability to respond favorably to new opportunities.

Unfortunately, there are many obstacles to commitment in society today—so many options, so many distractions, and so many excuses for not staying true to your commitments. These hindrances can challenge your resolve and often create rips in the fabric of our character. When character is weakened, destiny is also changed, usually for the worse.

There is power in commitment! Listen to the high regard that achievers have for the power of commitment:

Henry Emerson Fosdick, an American clergyman and author, wrote, "No steam or gas ever drives anything until it is confined. No Niagara is ever turned into light and power until it is tunneled. No life ever grows until it is focused, dedicated, and disciplined."

Walter Cronkite, the distinguished and now-retired news journalist, said, "I can't imagine a person becoming a success who doesn't give this game of life everything he's got."

Today, many of our heroes are sports figures. Often their stories are examples of the power of commitment. Dick Vermeil, now coach of the Kansas City Chiefs, summed up his feelings about commitment by saying, "If you don't invest very much, then defeat doesn't hurt very much and winning is not very exciting."

A legend in American football, the late Vince Lombardi expressed his feelings about commitment this way: "There is only one way to succeed in anything and that is to give everything. I do and I demand that my players do. Any man's finest hour is when he has worked his heart out in a good cause and lies exhausted on the field of battle . . . victorious." What a vivid picture of commitment!

Of course, the power of commitment does not limit itself to men either. Think of Mary Kay Ash, who started a new business in 1963 with $5,000 and a vision for how she could give women unlimited opportunity. The power of her commitment led to what has become the largest direct seller of skin care products in the United States today. With more than four hundred thousand sales representatives, her $5,000 investment has grown into a business that does more than $1 billion in sales each year!

Mary Kay knew something of the significance of television preacher Robert Schuller's statement about commitment.

He said, "Irrevocable commitments that offer no loopholes, no bail-out provisions, and no parachute clauses will extract incredible productivity and performance."

This statement reminds me of Hernando Cortés, the Spanish conqueror of Mexico in the early 1500s. When Cortés first landed near the site of Veracruz on April 21, 1519, he taught his men a lesson about the power of commitment. To prevent all thought of retreat, he burned his ships. Leaving a small force on the coast, Cortés led the remainder of his soldiers into the interior, where they were engaged in battles with the warlike Tlaxcalan Indians, and were outnumbered three hundred to one! And after three battles, these Indians became allies of Cortés and his men— because of the power of his commitment. Do you think those men would have had this same degree of commitment if their boats were still anchored in the harbor?

I wonder what new allies we would attract if we approached commitment with the same degree of determination that Cortés demonstrated. What power would be released into your life if you decided that, from this day forward, you would never make another commitment without a deliberate decision to absolutely fulfill it?

My favorite quote on the power of commitment comes from Johann Wolfgang van Goethe, a poet and playwright with as much significance in Germany as Shakespeare had in England:

> Until one is committed there is hesitancy, the chance to draw back, always ineffectiveness. Concerning all acts of initiation (and creation) there is one elementary truth, the ignorance of which kills countless ideas and splendid plans. That the moment one definitely commits oneself then providence moves too. All sort of things occur to help one that

would never otherwise have occurred. A whole stream of events issues from the decision raising in one's favor all manner of unforeseen incidents and meetings and material assistance which no man could have dreamt should come his way. Whatever you can do or dream, you can begin it. Boldness has genius, power and magic in it. Begin it now!

Vision, goals, choice, and commitment—these are the ultimate diamonds of the mind. When you discover them within and learn how to cut and polish them, they will bring you acres and acres of diamonds!

Action Steps

1. Make a list of the top five commitments you have made and how they have affected your life.

2. Identify one commitment you can make today that you know will improve your life, write it down, sign it, and give it to your closest friend so he or she can help you fulfill it.

3. Identify one great commitment that, if you stick with it, will dramatically change your life and help you fulfill your most ambitious vision.

Points to Ponder

"Anyone can dabble, but once you've made that commitment, then your blood has that particular thing in it, and it's very hard for people to stop you." — Bill Cosby

"There's a difference between interest and commitment. When you're interested in doing something, you do it only when it's convenient. When you're committed to

something, you accept no excuses, only results." — Kenneth
Blanchard

Part II
Diamonds of the Heart

"Above all else, guard your heart, for it is the wellspring of life."
— Proverbs 4:23

"A good heart is worth gold."
— William Shakespeare

Chapter 10
Desire

"Most of the significant things done in the world were done
by persons either too busy or too sick! There are few ideal
and leisurely settings for the disciplines of growth."
— Robert Thornton Henderson, Presbyterian theologian

Strong desire is a potent thing. No adult can ignore the power
with which a favorite child or grandchild can turn the course
of events or add to his possessions with a captivating smile
and strong desire. Those children particularly predisposed to
using desire as a tool in their quest of fulfillment are often called
"strongwilled." When they are young we vacillate between
considering this a character strength and a dangerous flaw to
be corrected. However, anyone who has ever achieved
anything of lasting significance has demonstrated this same
tenacity.

When it comes to the pursuit of dreams, strong desire is the
highest-rated fuel for success. Virtually all lasting change and
personal development begins with strong desire. We change a
habit, a job, or a vision for our lives when our desire for change
exceeds the inertia of our current circumstances. Quitting
smoking, losing weight, starting an exercise program, or
launching a new business are all actions that are initiated from
a desire within. Our ability to follow through is almost always
dependent on the depth of that desire.

Strong desire is the resource we depend on to persist when
everyone else quits because of weariness. Many start the race
but few complete it; they lack strong desire, and thus it is too
convenient to redefine their commitments during tough times.
Often those around us misunderstand our goals and dreams.
They either question the reasonableness of our dreams or they
resent our attempts to break free from the inertia they have
accepted as inevitable. Because they don't see what we see or
feel our desire, they criticize and often ridicule our new steps

toward freedom.

Strong desire frightens some people. It confronts another strong emotion that seeks to control their destiny: fear of failure. For some folks the battle between the two emotions is too great and they surrender to the feelings of inadequacy and low self-esteem. For those willing to risk, however, the strong desire for a clearly defined dream or goal empowers them to ignore their feelings of inadequacy and find a way to succeed. Strong desire is a great tool we can use to bring about change. It can bring us the rich and transforming treasures of courage, wisdom, strength, endurance, accomplishment, and ultimately, fulfillment.

Unfortunately, the vast majority of people never allow passion to lift them higher because they give too much credit to outside forces of resistance. They never discover the acres of diamonds that are available to those who nurture strong, purposeful desire that is built on ethical principles, nurtured by a vivid imagination, and focused through definite, measurable goals. The real winners in life are not those with the most talent, the highest education, or the greatest opportunities. They are those who are propelled into dynamic, exciting experiences as a result of a driving desire and unending pursuit of their dreams.

How can you develop the kind of powerful desire that will transform your future? It is found in developing an emotional expression of your mission. Mission starts with determining what you deeply care about and want to accomplish through your life. An emotionally powerful mission statement is simple, yet meaningful. Begin by writing several paragraphs about what is most important to you, and then look for a succinct, passionate way to communicate the core of your purpose through one phrase.

Here are some examples of mission statements:

- To continuously improve the lives of those I love
- To experience and reflect the glory of God in every area of my life

- To pursue the best and noblest in personal achievement
- To attain excellence and become the best in

_____

- To create a life of unconditional love

In and of themselves, none of the phrases listed above will create deep desire, but when they capture the heart of your mission they become an emotional expression of the empowering desire within. It is this deep treasure of desire that crafts a future of greatness that creates a unique journey for you.

Action Steps

1. Spend thirty minutes journaling about what is most important in your life. What values do you hold most dear? What kind of person do you want to become? What meaningful contributions do you want to make to the world around you? What kind of lifestyle do you want to enjoy and share with your loved ones? By answering these questions of what you want to be, do, and have, you can build a foundation for developing strong desire in your life. (Refer to your journaling action step in Chapter 4 and further develop these themes with emotion-packed descriptions.)

2. Finding a quiet place where you won't be distracted, begin to stir your imagination to see yourself emblazoned with passion for some noble purpose. What are you doing? Where are you doing it? How would you describe this passion that you observe?

3. Make a list of ten actions you can take to begin to pursue this passion today. Choose one to three of these items and plan how to integrate these actions into your life immediately.

Points to Ponder

"I believe in the power of desire backed by faith, because I have seen this power lift men from lowly beginnings to places of power and wealth; I have seen it rob the grave of its victims; I have seen it serve as the medium by which men staged a comeback after having been defeated in a hundred different ways. Through some strange and powerful principle of 'mental chemistry' which she has never divulged, Nature wraps up in the impulse of strong desire 'that something' which recognizes no such word as impossible, and accepts no such reality as failure." — Napoleon Hill

"Of all our human resources, the most precious is the desire to improve." — Anonymous

"You do not succeed because you do not know what you want, but because you don't want it intensely enough." — Frank Crane, journalist

Chapter 11
Discontentment

What events in your life have provided the greatest motivation for change? What relationships have triggered your best growth as an individual? When are you more focused on creativity and finding new solutions? When do you find the inspiration to create and pursue an important goal?

All of these questions can be answered the same way: when you experience discontentment. Most of us are creatures of comfort and convenience. We instinctively work to create a routine that is predictable and that provides us with enough of what we want to make life enjoyable. We refer to this as our comfort zone. When this status quo is interrupted, for any reason, our immediate response is to work on restoring stability in our lives. Yet in our rush for security, we often miss a greater treasure waiting to be discovered in discontentment.

There are several areas of our lives where discontentment may exist. The first need that we seek to satisfy is physical. This includes food, rest, shelter, health, and safety. These are usually the most obvious sources of discontentment, and if we aren't satisfying these needs, they usually trump every other need. To satisfy these needs we need money—and even though many people wish life weren't so complicated by the need to earn and manage money, very little can be accomplished without it. Discontentment with finances is a tricky motivation for many people. Some get carried away over the pursuit of money, while others appear to be afraid of it. Yet whether you approach money as a tycoon or a monk, physical needs cannot be met without it, and discontentment with our physical circumstances nearly always leads to a pursuit of more money.

The second sphere of needs is social, or relational. We seek companionship, assistance, encouragement, and love in our relationships. In fact, aspiring to vitality and fulfillment in this area is often our greatest challenge, particularly in relationships in which we feel stuck, such as at work or home. When a relationship results in tension, misunderstanding, exploitation, and resentment, the "fight or flight" syndrome ensues. Discontentment with stressful or dysfunctional relationships is a powerful stimulus needed for change. Exercising the courage necessary to deal with uncomfortable circumstances, resulting in reconciliation or changes that can open up new possibilities for love, care, and understanding, is usually the offspring of discontentment.

Discontentment also works to stimulate our intellectual development. In each of us is an innate need to grow, explore, and learn. This need isn't as obvious or demanding as our physical and relational needs, but it is a prevailing force just the same. Unfortunately, too many people feed their mental appetites with intellectual "junk foods," such as current event magazines, trashy novels, and an endless lineup of useless television shows and movies, ending up addicted to cerebral stimulations that do little to create growth. (My wife sometimes refers to my late-night television viewing as my "drug of choice.")

Fourth, a subtle and sometime elusive discontentment operates in our lives to address unfulfilled spiritual needs. Everyone possesses a yearning to make a difference in the life of someone else. If we don't find and express this need to make a contribution, discontentment will result. Often, this is the most difficult need to identify because it seems paradoxical: we have a need (selfish) to contribute to the lives of others (unselfish). Yet many people who satisfy their physical, relational, and intellectual needs continue to live in quiet desperation because of a well-camouflaged spiritual discontentment. This dissatisfaction often serves in our search for God, for some greater purpose for our lives, or for an opportunity to make a lasting impact in the lives of others. Without this discontentment, we would end up moving through the seasons of life without the nobility of purpose that gives meaning to our existence.

Of course, any of these areas of discontentment can get out of balance, driving us to pursue one particular need beyond what is healthy or beneficial in our lives. However, without a reasonable amount of discontentment, we would never stretch beyond our comfort zones to discover new possibilities and to explore the almost limitless possibilities of our potential. That is why I am very grateful for the blessing of discontentment.

What about you? Are there some areas of discontentment in your life? If so, don't feel guilty or resentful. Instead, recognize the tremendous blessing of your discontentment and start developing a plan to use this as a catalyst for change.

Action Steps

1. Make a list of any areas in your life where you feel discontentment: physical, including financial, relational, intellectual, and spiritual.

2 Prioritize these discontentments according to their order of importance to you today.

3. Take the top three and journal about how discontentment in this area of your life can serve as a catalyst for change.

Points to Ponder

"Life is often ambiguous and untidy. There are always loose ends. It is sticky, hot, cold, lukewarm at times—and frequently messy and unmanageable. Most of life is somewhere in between, in the middle—amidst small frustrations and a lot of 'I don't know what to do next.'" — Tim Hansel, author

"If you want to move your greatest obstacle, realize that the obstacle is yourself—and that the time to act is now!" — Nido Qubein, motivational speaker and author

"Crisis can have value because it generates transformation." — John Sculley, author and business executive

Chapter 12
Pain

Unto the Prison House of Pain none willingly repair—
The bravest who an entrance gain
Reluctant linger there;
For Pleasure, passing by that door, stays not to cheer the
sight,
And Sympathy but muffles sound and banishes the light.
Yet in the Prison House of Pain things full of beauty blow—
Like Christmas roses, which attain
Perfection with the snow—
Love, entering, in his mild warmth the darkest shadows
melt,
And often, where the hush is deep, the waft of wings is felt.
Ah, me! The Prison House of Pain!—what lessons there are
bought!
Lessons of a sublimer strain
Than any elsewhere taught;
Amid its loneliness and bloom, grave meanings grow more
clear,
For to no earthly dwelling-place seems God so strangely
near!

— Florence Earle Coates

If discontentment is an inner voice clamoring for change, then pain is the trumpet blast. For acute pain, above all else, demands from us a response. We will do almost anything and go anywhere to get rid of acute pain. Whether physical, emotional, intellectual, or spiritual, acute pain dominates our existence until we find relief.

Having moved into middle age, I occasionally observe how much I'm willing to put up with chronic physical pain. I may wake up with aching muscles from the previous day's tennis match, or suffer with a dull headache from dehydration or tension, or tolerate an aching joint. Most of the time, I don't think anything of it. I just accept it as part of life, and, as long as it doesn't become acute, I wait for my body to resolve whatever the problem may be by itself. It seems that as we grow older, we condition ourselves to accept chronic pain and we learn to live with it as a reasonable part of life. Even when we do respond to acute physical pain, most of us show little concern for its cause as long as we can find immediate relief. After all, we don't take aspirin for a headache because we suffer from an aspirin deficiency!

I suspect the same principle follows suit in the other compartments of our lives, whether they are emotional, intellectual, or spiritual pains. (If we can have emotional, intellectual, and spiritual needs, then we can have pains in these areas also.) We may be vaguely aware of chronic pain in these areas from time to time, but for the most part we carry on without giving them much attention, anticipating that they will work themselves out over time. When they become acute we address them in such a manner as to eliminate the immediate crisis, but seldom do we probe deeper to uncover the underlying cause of our emotional, intellectual, or spiritual pains.

In many instances this wait-and-see approach is the best course of action. However, the medical advances of the last twenty-five years have taught us of another, more valuable purpose for pain. We have learned that pain is often the messenger of a deeper systemic problem that, if not addressed at the root cause, results in serious consequences.

When we have physical pain of increasing intensity, most of us employ graduated tactics of response. First, we take a rest. Then, we may attempt to self-medicate. If the pain is acute enough and persists, we visit our primary health care provider. Sometimes we are passed along to one or more specialists. The goal of this progression is first to eliminate the pain and, when it appears more serious, to identify and treat the underlying cause.

How often do you follow a similar blueprint when responding

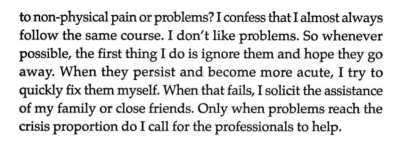

to non-physical pain or problems? I confess that I almost always follow the same course. I don't like problems. So whenever possible, the first thing I do is ignore them and hope they go away. When they persist and become more acute, I try to quickly fix them myself. When that fails, I solicit the assistance of my family or close friends. Only when problems reach the crisis proportion do I call for the professionals to help.

Most of us generally don't think of problems as friends. And we most assuredly don't refer to them as "hidden treasures"! Instead, they are irritations to be ignored or eliminated as soon as possible. But what if they are messengers of a deeper condition? What if they exist to teach us something of greater value? What if these problems have some resource contained within that produce diamonds in our lives that bring new wealth and beauty into existence?

Consider what sages have written about this pain we refer to as a problem:

In *Success through a Positive Mental Attitude*, Napoleon Hill wrote, "Every adversity, every failure and every heartache carries with it the seed of an equivalent or a greater benefit."

M. Scott Peck, author of *The Road Less Traveled*, wrote, "It is in the whole process of meeting and solving problems that life has meaning. Problems are the cutting edge that distinguishes between success and failure. Problems call forth our courage and our wisdom; indeed, they create our courage and our wisdom. It is only because of problems that we grow mentally and spiritually. It is through the pain of confronting and resolving problems that we learn."

This is not my normal response to problems. I intellectually accept that problems are a part of life. I also acknowledge that problems stimulate growth by teaching us new ways of doing things. But ask me if I would rather have a life free of problems or one saturated with them, and I will quickly choose the former, thinking that I'm doing myself a favor.

If problems really do contain treasure, how are we to uncover it? And how can we convert this pain into gain? I believe the answer to these two questions lies in learning to analyze problems and then tap into the energy compressed in them, which, if released, will bring significant change.

First, instead of minimizing or brushing aside a problem, we need to intensify it, define it, and get to the core of it. As with physical pain, our first instinct is to fixate on the symptom. We just want the symptom to go away, not caring about or searching for the cause. It is only after the symptoms persist that we start to probe deeper. Even then, it is only when we intensify our awareness of the problem by uncovering and expressing the personal impact of our problem that we release the energy pent up for its resolution.

I have discovered much about this search for the treasures in pain through a sales training course offered by Crossroads Training & Business Development of Boise, Idaho. Jim Stephens, the owner of Crossroads, teaches an approach to problem solving called a "pain funnel." It proceeds like this:

1. What is the biggest problem you are having with _____?
2. Tell me more about that.
3. Can you be a bit more specific, maybe give me an example?
4. How long has that been a problem?
5. What have you tried to do to solve it?
6. Why do you suppose that didn't work?
7. How has this problem affected you directly?
8. How does that make you feel?
9. Are you ready to give up trying to deal with it?
10. Is there anything else about this problem that would be helpful to understand?
11. What are you hoping to do about this problem?
12. What action steps will that require?

Jim's questions begin by identifying symptoms, or the surface indicators. Through the questioning process, the funnel moves into the underlying causes for the problem. Then the questions uncover the personal impact, which is the compressed energy core for making change. Finally, as this emotional energy for change is opened up, Jim asks his clients what actions steps should be engaged to resolve the problem or harvest its greatest purpose. Jim affectionately refers to himself as a "pain-seeking missile" because of the power he has discovered this process releases into a person's life. I have found this method very effective in unlocking the "equivalent or greater benefit" found in problems.

Jim's pain funnel reminds me of a problem-solving blueprint that Fred Smith, founder of Federal Express, suggests: "Find the essence of each situation, like a logger clearing a logjam. The pro climbs a tall tree and locates the key log, blows it, and lets the stream do the rest. An amateur would start at the edge of the jam and move all the logs, eventually moving the key log. Both approaches work, but the 'essence' concept saves time and effort. Almost all problems have a 'key' log if we learn to find it."

What pains hold treasures for you? What problems have become acute enough that you are ready to quit tolerating them and start taking action to overcome them? Instead of ignoring or denying pain, why not allow it to enrich your life by unleashing the power within?

Action Steps

1. Choose an area of discontentment and "unpack your pain" through journaling, using the pain funnel questions listed in this chapter. You will know you have effectively unpacked your pain when you begin to reach a deep emotional response.

2. Listen to your heart and pray for an answer to the problem you have journaled about. You will know you have found your answer when it is something for which you can take responsibility. As long as you think someone else has to initiate

something, you still don't have the right answer.

3. List the action steps you will take immediately to engage the emotional energy unleashed by unpacking your problem.

Points to Ponder

"The best years of your life are the ones in which you decide your problems are your own. You don't blame them on your mother, the ecology or the president. You realize that you control your own destiny." — Albert Ellis, clinical psychologist

"Those things that hurt, instruct." — Benjamin Franklin

"This tendency to avoid problems and the emotional suffering inherent in them is the primary basis of all human mental illness." — Charles Swindoll, pastor and author

Chapter 13
Enthusiasm

Henry Chester called it "the greatest asset in the world." He said it "beats money, power and influence." Ralph Waldo Emerson said that every great and commanding movement in the history of the world was as a result of it. Emory Ward likened it to "measles, mumps, and the common cold; it's highly contagious." J. Paul Getty ranked it ahead of imagination, business acumen, and ambition. What is it? The power of enthusiasm!

Edward Butler wrote, "Every man is enthusiastic at times. One man has enthusiasm for 30 minutes—another man has it for 30 days, but it is the man who has it for 30 years who makes a success of life." What is this quality of character, this magic we call "enthusiasm"?

The word comes from the Greek *entheos,* which means to be "in god." It's an inner flame of excitement that causes us to hold our heads up, to walk a little quicker and a little lighter, and to flash that sparkle in our eyes. Charles Kingsley said, "We act as though comfort and luxury were the chief requirements of life, when all that we need to make us happy is something to be enthusiastic about."

But for enthusiasm to be real, it can't be a gimmick. It can't be a mask we put on to make other people think everything is going okay on the inside. For enthusiasm to have its way in our lives, it must be genuine and personal. We must make sure we aspire to accomplish something worth accomplishing, and then we should throw our whole energy into it. What's worth doing is worth doing well. And to do anything well, we have to give it our all, including our enthusiasm.

For me, enthusiasm begins by careful contemplation. I ask myself, "Is this project or this goal I am contemplating something I can stay excited about long enough to complete?

Is it worthy of my devotion, my energy, and my resources? Is it worth everything it will take to overcome the obstacles I'm bound to run into along the way?" If the answer is yes, then its time for me to get excited and to stay excited no matter what comes my way.

Please don't misinterpret what I am saying. To tap the power of enthusiasm doesn't require a lifetime commitment, unless the goal is a lifetime goal. You can practice enthusiasm even in the most ordinary things, and the immense power of enthusiasm can work wonders for you. You can clean the basement with an attitude of drudgery and it can be one of the longest days of your life. Or you can choose to be enthusiastic about what the basement is going to look like when you are finished and find joy in otherwise unpleasant work.

Henry David Thoreau used to lie in bed for a while in the morning telling himself all the good news he could think of: that he had a healthy body, that his mind was alert, that his work was interesting, that the future looked bright, that a lot of people trusted him. He then arose to meet the day in a world filled with good things, good people, and good opportunities. He activated enthusiasm before beginning his day. In that way, Thoreau took responsibility for his own level of enthusiasm throughout the day.

As a young boy I remember a relative who was respected by our family because of his cool, reserved demeanor. He was quiet, never showed much emotion, and tended to respond to excitement with skepticism and a slightly sarcastic sense of humor. I can remember wanting to be like him when I grew up because he seemed to be cool and "in control." Now, after fifty years of living, I have concluded it was poor judgment on my part to want to emulate his approach to life. Instead, I've decided to be a kid again, to get excited about the great things happening in my life, and to stay excited about my vision for a continuously improving future. I want to get excited about a beautiful sunrise coming over the mountains, reflecting off the lake on the back deck of our home. I want to get excited about the brilliance of the stars on a warm summer night. I want to get excited about the privilege of growing, loving relationships with my children. And I want to get excited about making my work important by focusing my efforts on making a difference in the lives of others. Thomas Huxley said, "The secret of genius is to carry the spirit of the child into old age, which means never losing your enthusiasm."

If enthusiasm isn't the dominant emotion rising from your heart every morning, there are ways you can change. Make a deliberate decision to turn away from negative thoughts, attitudes, and behaviors that steal a continuous expectation for good in your life. Retrain your mind to focus on positive, admirable thoughts and attitudes. And act enthusiastic, for our emotions cannot hold two opposites at the same time. If you act enthusiastic, in time you will be enthusiastic.

But don't try to use enthusiasm to impress others. This is insincere and it will backfire. Instead, make it your goal to build enthusiasm within yourself. This deep, heart-generated enthusiasm will come out naturally, genuinely, to make you more attractive and interesting to others. Whom would you rather be with—someone who exudes vitality, enthusiasm, and a zest for life, or a pessimistic, downtrodden bore? When given the choice, the majority of people from all walks of life would rather befriend the optimistic, enthusiastic, upbeat person.

If you want to supercharge your enthusiasm, follow the advice of Napoleon Hill and W. Clement Stone in *Success through a Positive Mental Attitude*. They challenge their readers to develop a "magnificent obsession" to spend their lives on. The core of this magnificent obsession is to develop a burning desire to be helpful to others, regardless of what you receive in return. As you make it an obsession to serve others, enthusiasm will burst forth and you will discover that most of your problems will come into clear focus, allowing you to gain an objective understanding of their cause and what you can do to alleviate or minimize their impact on your life.

Enthusiasm is a continuously renewable resource: the more you draw on it, the more you will have. It will find solutions where there appear to be none. And it will achieve success when success was thought impossible.

The late Norman Vincent Peale, one of the most prolific writers about enthusiasm, offered these ten steps for how to nurture enthusiasm in your life:

1. Look for interest and romance in the simple things.
2. Enlarge your view of your own God-given capabilities. Within the limit of humility develop a good opinion of yourself.
3. Diligently practice eliminating all dull, dead, unhealthy thoughts so that your mind may be freshened up and capable of developing enthusiasm.
4. Daily affirm enthusiasm. As you think it, talk it, and live it, you will have it.
5. Practice daily relaxation to keep your mind and spirit from getting tired.
6. Act enthusiastic for as you act, you will tend to be.
7. Allow no sense of guilt to take the luster off your spirit.
8. Keep the creative channel open between you and God.
9. Keep spiritually virile and alive.
10. Give all you've got to life and it will give its greatest gifts to you. It will never grow dull.

The irresistible power of enthusiasm . . . make sure you get your fill of it today!

Action Steps

1. In one sentence, write out your "magnificent obsession," that one statement of purpose that causes your heart to fill with hope and enthusiasm.

2. Write an affirmation that expresses your commitment to live life with enthusiasm, such as, "I am enthusiastic about my life because _____."

3. Fasten a copy of this affirmation to the sun visor in your car or somewhere else where you will see it several times every

day. Create a routine that prompts you to read this affirmation aloud at least ten times a day. For example, before I step out of my car, I read the affirmation out loud, and then I unfasten my seat belt and open the door.

Points to Ponder

"People who are unable to motivate themselves must be content with mediocrity, no matter how impressive their other talents." — Andrew Carnegie

"No one keeps his enthusiasm automatically. Enthusiasm must be nourished with new action, new aspirations, new efforts, and new vision. It is one's own fault if enthusiasm is gone." — Papyrus

Chapter 14
Perseverance

Sir Winston Churchill took three years to pass eighth grade because he had trouble learning English. Ironically, years later Oxford University asked him to address its commencement exercises. He arrived with his usual props: a cigar, a cane, and a top hat, which accompanied Churchill wherever he went. As Churchill approached the podium, the crowd rose in appreciative applause. With unmatched dignity, he settled the crowd and stood confident before his admirers. Removing the cigar from his mouth and carefully placing the top hat on the podium, Churchill gazed at his waiting audience. Authority rang in Churchill's voice as he shouted, "Never give up!" Several seconds passed before he rose to his toes and repeated, "Never give up!" His words thundered in their ears. There was a deafening silence as Churchill reached for his hat and cigar, steadied himself with his cane, and left the platform. His commencement address was finished.

There is probably no better example than Winston Churchill of the inner power of perseverance. But there are still many other good examples. For instance, twenty-three publishers rejected Dr. Seuss's first children's book. The twenty-fourth publisher sold six million copies and Dr. Seuss died knowing his perseverance resulted in entertaining, challenging, and educating millions of children.

Henry Ford went bankrupt twice during his first three years in the automobile business, but he didn't give up. Vince Lombardi didn't become a head coach in the NFL until he was forty-seven. Michelangelo endured seven years of lying on his back on a scaffold to paint the Sistine Chapel. Charles Goodyear was obsessed with the idea of making rubber unaffected by temperature extremes. Years of unsuccessful experimentation caused bitter disappointment, imprisonment for debt, family difficulties, and ridicule from friends. He persevered and in February 1839, Goodyear discovered that adding sulfur to rubber achieved his purpose.

In 1902, the poetry editor of the *Atlantic Monthly* returned the poems of a twenty-eight- year-old poet with the following note: "Our magazine has no room for your vigorous verse." Robert Frost persevered. In 1905, the University of Bern rejected a doctoral dissertation, saying that it was irrelevant and fanciful. Albert Einstein was disappointed but not defeated. He persevered. And one of my favorite examples of perseverance involves a man who didn't seem to understand his limitations and who continuously reached higher than his colleagues thought appropriate. He:

> Failed in business at the age of 22,
> Was defeated for the state legislature at the age of 23,
> Failed again in business at the age of 24,
> Was elected to the legislature at the age of 25,
> Lost his sweetheart to death at the age of 26,
> Had a nervous breakdown at the age of 27,
> Lost an election for speaker of the legislature at the age of 29,
> Lost an election to become an elector at the age of 31,
> Was defeated for the House of Representatives at the age of 34,
> Was elected to the House of Representatives at the age of 37,
> Was defeated for the House of Representatives at the age of 39,
> Was defeated for the Senate at the age of 46,
> Was defeated for the vice presidency at the age of 47,
> Was defeated again for the Senate at the age of 49,
> And was elected president of the United States at the age of 51.

That's the resume of Abraham Lincoln! Imagine what courage and perseverance it must have taken to endure so many defeats and still keep marching in the direction of his vision for his life. The list above probably isn't all of them. These are just the "public" defeats he endured that everyone around him knew about.

And the stories go on and on. In case after case, perseverance was a vital ingredient for success and greatness.

John D. Rockefeller said, "I do not think there is any other quality so essential to success of any kind as the quality of perseverance. It overcomes almost everything, even nature." Johann Wolfgang von Goethe wrote, "Austere perseverance, harsh and continuous, may be employed by the smallest of us and rarely fails of its purpose, for its silent power grows irresistibly greater with time." And Jacob A. Riis wrote, "When nothing else seems to help, I go and look at a stonecutter hammering away at his rock, perhaps a hundred times without as much as a crack showing in it. Yet, at the hundred and first blow, it will split in two, and I know it was not that blow that did it, but all that had gone before."

Harriet Beecher Stowe said it this way: "When you get into a tight place and everything goes against you, til it seems that you could not hold on a minute longer, never give up then for that is just the place and time that the tide will turn." And President Calvin Coolidge wrote, "Nothing in the world can take the place of persistence. Talent will not; nothing is more common than unsuccessful people with talent. Genius will not; unrewarded genius is almost a proverb. Education will not; the world is full of educated derelicts. Persistence and determination alone are omnipotent."

In spite of all the compelling stories and quotes about perseverance, it is still one of the rare qualities in society today. Granted, most of us don't give up in dramatic ways—instead, we usually find quiet, subtle ways to turn away from our dreams of greatness, to settle for a life of convenience and mediocrity. Sometimes our compromise is so subtle that even we don't realize we have taken the lesser road and lost the zeal for greatness that once captured our imaginations. We have stopped the faithful execution of the activities, the discipline, and the perseverance necessary to bring our dreams to reality.

Several years ago, I became curious about the antithesis of perseverance and how prevalent it seems to have become in our society. I was surprised to learn that almost everyone thinks about quitting. Employees often think about quitting their jobs, business owners often think about quitting (or selling) their businesses, pastors and priests often think about quitting the ministry, politicians often think about quitting public service, and couples often think about quitting their marriages.

In almost every instance I discovered that the primary reason people seriously consider quitting is because they come to view themselves as victims. They feel that outside forces of one type or another make it too difficult for them to continue to pursue their dreams. Employees complain about bosses and company policies that conflict with their values. Business owners complain about competition and over-regulation. Religious leaders complain about complacency and the pressures of performing in ministry. Politicians complain about media and campaign demands. And couples complain about dysfunctional relationships or lost romance. In every instance, the common thread is the onset of a victim mentality, that feeling of powerlessness against external forces that have destroyed the idealism that once guided a strong sense of purpose.

Of course, there are some instances where giving up *is* the appropriate thing to do. If and when we realize the target we set for our lives is wrong, or others we love are being hurt by our perseverance, the noble thing to do may be to quit. Maybe our purpose has lost its moral integrity through a series of mistakes and poor judgment, or demands from others have emerged that challenge us to compromise our character and ethical core in order to continue. These are all legitimate reasons to quit and rethink our goals and dreams. Rarely, however, are these the reasons people quit.

Usually, we drift away from our goals and commitments because their fulfillment is more difficult than we originally envisioned. It's taking us longer than we expected, we aren't getting the results as easily as we hoped, or we discover we don't have all the skills we need to achieve our goals. Sometimes we drift because of criticism from others or, worse yet, because of self-criticism that decimates our self-confidence. Maybe we become discouraged because others have let us down. Or maybe we didn't realize the pursuit of our goals was going to be an uphill journey—all the way! Even though these are the most common reasons why people cease to persevere, none of them are good reasons to quit.

How can you reinvigorate your resolve? How can you stay the course until you have truly won the race? I suggest three steps to strengthen your ability to persevere. If practiced regularly, and by that I mean daily and weekly, these three steps can help keep you from discouragement and strengthen your inner resolve to achieve something great beyond your present experience, and maybe even beyond your current imagination.

First, you can strengthen your ability to persevere through the renewal of your vision. Keeping the big picture in mind and reviewing it regularly will remind you that whatever price you have to pay is worth it. You can do this through a life mission statement and a set of lifetime goals.

Second, you can strengthen your perseverance "muscle" through a sharper focus. To focus is to center your attention on those activities that are most likely to help you fulfill your vision. In order to do this, you also must learn to close out every distraction that competes for this intensity of focus. In today's world, a major cause for drifting is the multitude of activities, interests, and sensory stimulations competing for your energies. To focus is to consciously and deliberately choose those activities that will move you forward in your dreams and to intentionally say no to all others.

The third step to deepen perseverance is to cultivate the habit of thankfulness daily. Why, you may ask, would thankfulness be so important to perseverance? Because thankfulness is the greatest weapon we have in the battle against discouragement, which is almost always the root reason why people quit. Eliminate discouragement, and you have conquered the single greatest cause of failure! I have discovered an amazing truth—

that a person cannot hold two opposite attitudes or emotions at the same time. We have been designed to experience only one at a time. For instance, you can't be happy and angry simultaneously. In order to experience one, you have to give up the other. So, if you make a daily habit of cultivating thankfulness, if you are constantly looking for new reasons to be thankful, and if you learn to be genuinely thankful in every circumstance, there will no longer be any room for discouragement.

Perseverance is another diamond of the heart because it is a resource that you will never find anywhere else—it comes only from your heart. And it is there, waiting to be brought forth to carry you to success.

Don't Quit

When things go wrong, as they sometimes will,
When the road you're trudging seems all uphill,
When the funds are low and the debts are high,
And you want to smile, but you have to sigh,
When care is pressing you down a bit,
Rest, if you must—but don't you quit.

Life is queer with its twists and turns,
As every one of us sometimes learns,
And many a failure turns about
When he might have won had he stuck it out;
Don't give up, though the pace seems slow—
You might succeed with another blow.

Often the goal is nearer than
It seems to a faint and faltering man,
Often the struggler has given up
When he might have captured the victor's cup.
And he learned too late, when the night slipped down,
How close he was to the golden crown.

Success is failure turned inside out—
The silver tint of the clouds of doubt—
And you never can tell how close you are,

It may be near when it seems afar;
So stick to the fight when you're hardest hit—
It's when things seem worst that you mustn't quit.

— Clinton Howell

Action Steps

1. Make a list of times in the past when you persevered through challenges and gained a great reward because you didn't quit.

2. Make a list of difficulties you are currently facing that are challenging your will to persevere.

3. Make a list of all the benefits you will enjoy if you persevere in your current challenges.

Points to Ponder

"Diamonds are pieces of coal that stuck to their jobs in spite of the heat and pressure." — Anonymous

"We all have moments when we feel better than our best, and we say, 'I feel fit for anything; if only I could be like this always!' We are not meant to be. We must bring our commonplace life up to the standard revealed in the high hour. Never allow a feeling which was stirred in you in the high hour to evaporate."
— Oswald Chambers

Chapter 15
Listening

Are you interested in developing one skill that is guaranteed to improve every other aspect of your life? This skill can affect everything from your success in business to your closest relationships and happiness. It is a simple skill, but not necessarily easy. It is challenging, but the rewards for making it a central part of your life are immeasurable. It is the most important skill used by everyone from a concert violinist or a top salesperson. It will turn enemies into friends, skeptics into believers, and product presentations into profitable sales.

What is it, you ask? Believe it or not, it's something that almost all of us were born with, naturally. It is one of the first skills we begin to develop as babies and, sadly, it is also one of the easiest skills to lose without constant practice. This wonderful, challenging, tremendously rewarding skill that I am speaking of is the skill of listening.

Listening and understanding others is the cornerstone on which every truly professional person builds his success. Yet it is also one of the primary stumbling blocks for those who have not yet learned its importance.

So many benefits come to a highly advanced listener. When you polish this diamond into one of your greatest strengths, you will see a whole new world that you didn't realize existed before. Other people will suddenly enjoy being around you; they will readily share their needs with you and reveal many ways that you can fulfill your goals by serving them. Because your intent listening shows them how much you care, they will take new interest in what you know. In addition, when they know that you have listened and understood them deeply, they won't feel as if you are just trying to sell them something or control them. Probably the greatest benefit of all is that you yourself will be changed by listening effectively to others.

When Charles Wang's family arrived in America in 1949, they had two suitcases. Today, Wang is worth more than $100 million in Computer Associates International stock. Wang said that most computer companies sell people what they need; he decided to ask them what they wanted and then listen. Automotive experts are in full agreement that the Japanese automakers gained significant market share in the United States because while Detroit was telling customers what they should want, the Japanese were asking what they wanted. These are business examples of the treasures uncovered through listening more effectively, but I believe the same principle holds true in any interaction between people, from families to friends to factories.

Of course, any skill can be executed correctly or incorrectly. So what are some of the mistakes we make in listening to others? Probably the biggest is when we "listen to respond." This means that instead of patiently considering and feeling what another person is saying, we immediately begin formulating our response in our minds while they are speaking. We then take the first available opportunity to interrupt and begin vocalizing our thoughts. This approach to listening creates more frustration than anything else. The person we speak to walks away, thinking that we don't care enough to listen closely. This causes him to conclude that we haven't understood his concerns sufficiently enough to help him in any significant way.

The second mistake in listening comes when we listen to argue. This is very similar to listening to respond, but a little more aggressive. Maybe we take the time to listen to all that the other person is saying, but our motive is to find a vulnerable spot in his position so that we can win a debate or prove our superior mental capacities or control the conversation in order to get our way. When we approach listening this way, we fail to see the deeper purpose in communicating. Our ability to influence or persuade others is anchored in our ability to first understand their point of view and the reasons they feel the way they do.

The third mistake we make is when we listen to what is being said autobiographically. This means that we allow the words we hear to trigger similar memories and we then link the speaker's communication to our own experiences. This type of listening is exposed by phrases like, "I know what you mean. That is the same thing that happened to me when . . . ." But do we really know that it is the same thing? Our situation may be similar to the speaker's, but it can never be exactly the same. When we make this autobiographical link, we are turning down a greater opportunity to understand what was unique about the other person's experience. This kind of listening also causes us to respond to people condescendingly, making them feel once again as if we haven't really heard what they wanted us to understand.

History teaches us that Winston Churchill's greatest attribute was his bulldogged stubbornness. However, those close to him often remarked at what an effective listener he was. He never cut off a suggestion with a curt dismissal but encouraged elaboration in order to gain a deeper understanding of why the person speaking to him felt as he did. In *The 7 Habits of Highly Effective People*, Stephen Covey writes, "If you really seek to understand, without hypocrisy and without guile, there will be times when you will be literally stunned with the pure knowledge and understanding that will flow to you from another human being."

How can we improve our skills as listeners? How can we change the habits and patterns that compromise our listening skills and become more valuable and useful to others? There are some simple steps we can take that will help us grow bigger ears and hearts, empowering us to become more valuable to others and, in turn, increasing our own happiness and success.

The first step to better listening is to be able to repeat what the other person has said to you. It may seem silly to do this, but it is a surefire way to break the bad habit of listening to respond. I often use this exercise when counseling with people who are, by nature, antagonists. I have discovered that it is much harder to fight when you have to listen closely enough to repeat the words the other person has just spoken. A useful way to do this is to begin with, "Let me tell you what I'm hearing and then you can tell me if I have it right or not." By repeating the exact words you hear as closely as possible, you increase your listening capacity. Of course, it may not always be appropriate to repeat what you have heard word-for-word. However, this discipline will help you focus your attention more on listening and less on how you want to respond.

After achieving a measure of success with this kind of listening, the next step is to repeat the content of what is being said using different words. This forces you to take another step in the listening process. It teaches you to think through the content of what the person is saying. It also helps to demonstrate your sincere desire to understand him thoroughly before responding. Once again, it will impede autobiographical listening and heighten your senses to information that may have otherwise gone unnoticed.

The next step in quality listening is to repeat the feeling of the other person. It isn't enough to just hear words, or even to be able to change the words without losing content. It is only when we begin to hear the heart that we truly begin to hear the whole person. What sort of emotions is the person feeling? How are these being expressed? Are deeper needs being revealed beyond the words? These are all questions to use in order to identify more closely with what is unique in his experience.

Finally, answer the following questions to determine how well you have listened. First, has the other person satisfied his need to talk? Has he received the "emotional oxygen" that comes from being heard thoroughly? Is he asking for a response? If not, then he probably doesn't feel you have listened enough yet. One of my greatest temptations is to tell others that I already know what they want to say. I fall into the delusion of thinking that I can read their mind and I know what they are trying to say even before the words come forth. I usually communicate this in subtle, sometimes nonverbal ways, but the message is quite clear: "I understand what you are trying to tell me—now I want you to listen to me so I can share my great wisdom with you." But I have found this is rarely true. I may know certain aspects about what they are communicating, but unless I take the time to hear them at a heart level (which is indicated by engagement at an emotional level), I understand only a small portion of what I should. Even if I do know what they want to say, they still need to say it! Effective listening demands patience.

Second, could you be an effective advocate for the other person's point of view? It doesn't matter whether you agree or disagree with what he is saying. Do you understand it well enough that he would trust you to represent his position to another person? This is a valuable exercise in selling, negotiating, and reconciling differences. Most often, people think we disagree because we don't fully understand them. If we can show that we understand well enough to represent their position, they often will be more open to being influenced by a different opinion. Many times our listening and probing for deeper understanding will result in others discovering deeper truth without us saying anything. And, as Ralph Waldo Emerson said, "Every man I meet is in some way my superior, and I can learn of him."

Action Steps

1. Who are the best listeners in your life? Journal about what makes them such good listeners.

2. Make a list of three people whom you want to listen to deeply over the next seven days. Tell them you are working to improve your listening skills. Use questions to engage them in conversation and keep telling yourself, "I don't really understand yet," as a way of going deeper.

3. Develop the practice of repeating back what you are hearing, beginning by reflecting the words, then the content, and finally the feelings you are hearing, asking for confirmation or correction from the person you are listening to.

Points to Ponder

"Big people monopolize the listening. Small people monopolize the talking." — David Schwartz, author of *The Magic of Thinking Big*

"The head has not heard until the heart has listened."
— Anonymous

Chapter 16
Friendship

I took a sabbatical during the year 2000 while transitioning between careers. For the summer months, one of my goals (much to my wife's chagrin) was to finally learn how to play golf. I mean *really* play golf. I bought two highly recommended instruction books, spent a considerable amount of time at the driving range, and had a standing golf appointment with a good friend every Monday morning while everyone else was beginning a new week of work.

Occasionally, I would play a round all by myself—just because I wanted to play and everyone else was at work. One quiet, midweek afternoon I was playing the eleventh hole of my favorite course, hitting my third shot on a very difficult par four that I don't think I had ever played better than a plus five. My shot was approximately eighty-five yards from the hole and I chose a pitching wedge and swung away, hoping to land on or near the green. My ball took a steep ascent toward the green and, much to my amazement, plummeted into the hole without ever touching the green. I was dumbfounded! I dropped my golf club in amazement and wondered, *What do I do now?* Without a doubt, it was the most remarkable moment in my mediocre attempts at golf, and there I stood—alone. Nobody saw what happened but me. Nobody was there to cheer for me. And nobody watched me walk up to the hole, bend down, and pull the ball out of the hole while the flagstick remained in place.

This is one of the more memorable, albeit frivolous, examples from my life about the value of friendship. We have all experienced more significant times when friendship was precious to us—either when celebrating some great milestone in our lives, or mourning a painful loss, or just sitting on the deck on a warm summer evening reminiscing about old times. What good are all the other treasures that come to us throughout our lives without companionship? In his book,

When All You've Ever Wanted Isn't Enough, Harold Kushner wrote, "A life without people, without the same people day after day, people who belong to us, people who will be there for us, people who need us and whom we need in return, may be very rich in other things, but in human terms, it is not life at all."

Friendship truly is a prized diamond of the heart. It has been described as a "treasure ship anyone can launch." Seth Parker wrote,

> The happiest business in all the world is that of making friends,
> And no investment on the street pays larger dividends,
> For life is more than stocks and bonds, and love than rate percent,
> And he who gives in friendship's name shall reap what he has spent.

Friendship is not so much about finding people who will like and support you; instead, it is a treasure of the heart that empowers you to like and support them. Dale Carnegie said, "You can make more friends in two months by becoming interested in other people than in two years by trying to get other people interested in you."

One of the greatest "friends" I have ever met is a man named Charlie "Tremendous" Jones. He picked up the middle name "Tremendous" years ago on the speaking circuit because no matter what question you asked him, his answer was always, "Tremendous!" Charlie can count thousands of friends on almost every continent on earth. Why? Because Charlie Jones is a friend everywhere he goes—and it comes enthusiastically from his heart. He has discovered, cut, and polished this diamond to perfection, complete with big bear hugs for the men (don't worry, he insists he doesn't enjoy it any more than the men he embraces) and warm, passionate handshakes for the women. Charlie tells many stories to illustrate why, though most people consider him a little crazy and overbearing, he continues to express the heart of friendship with big hugs and bigger smiles. One of his favorite stories is about hugging and greeting hundreds of people after a talk one night in Minneapolis. Several weeks later he received a letter from an older man. He wrote to Charlie, "You will remember me—I'm the older gentleman you hugged after your speech in Minneapolis. I just wanted you to know that you are the first person who has ever hugged me my entire life." What a jewel you have discovered, Mr. Jones!

George Washington Carver wrote, "How far you go in life depends on your being tender with the young, compassionate with the aged, sympathetic with the striving, and tolerant of the weak and strong. Because someday in your life you will have been all of these."

What kind of a friend are you? Have you mined this hidden treasure? Here are some things to think about as you uncover friendship as a diamond of the heart:

Friendship is faithful. By listening, by caring, and by helping, you add strength and stability to another person's life.

Friendship is kind. By giving attention and encouragement that cannot be purchased, you validate a person's unique worth.

Friendship is loyal. By not talking behind a person's back differently than you speak of him in his presence, you esteem him.

Friendship is compassionate. By standing with a person through difficulty and loss, you help preserve him.

Friendship is forgiving. By not counting a person's transgressions against him, you help restore him.

Friendship is gentle. By reaching out to a person in trouble, you help redeem him.

Friendship is sacrificial. Jesus said, "Greater love has no one than this, that he lay down his life for his friends" (John 15:13).

Friendship is about giving—and the more you give it the more you will receive it. If you want to optimize the diamond of friendship in your heart, be a friend of more than those like yourself. Have some friends who are old and some who are young. Have some friends you look up to for guidance and some who do the same with you. Have some friends you work with and some you play with, some who listen and some who speak. Have liberal friends as well as conservative friends and some who come from different cultures and creeds as well. Finally, have friends whom you can feel safe with, having neither to weigh your thoughts nor measure your words when you are with them.

Abraham Lincoln was criticized by an associate for his attitude toward his enemies: "Why do you try to make friends of them? You should try to destroy them." Lincoln replied gently, "Am I not destroying my enemies when I make them my friends?" Another president, Richard Nixon, prophetically wrote, "Those who hate you don't win unless you hate them—and then you destroy yourself." So, to perfect your diamond of friendship, determine to be a friend to all and you will reap more treasure than you can ever spend!

Action Steps

1. Make a list of your ten best friends.

- What are their ages?
- In what ways are they different from you?
- What are their incomes?
- What are their talents?
- What are their dreams?
- What are their needs?

What does this list teach you?

2. Make a list of ten ways you can express friendship.

3. Become an anonymous friend every week by doing something

for someone you don't know that will never be discovered.

Points to Ponder

"The only way to have a friend is to be a friend." — Ralph Waldo Emerson

"One learns people through the heart, not the eyes or intellect." — Mark Twain

Part III
Diamonds of the Body

"For you created my inmost being; you knit me together in
my mother's womb. I praise you for I am fearfully and
wonderfully made."
(Psalms 139:13-14)

Chapter 17
The Digestive System

When it comes to caring for an automobile, most of us understand and respect the importance of proper use and maintenance. We readily accept that our cars were designed and manufactured to operate within specific scientific principles. For example, we realize the engine was designed to use a specific fuel and that if we violate this protocol there will be severe consequences, ranging from diminished performance to complete failure. We recognize that our cars require various types of maintenance at certain intervals and, if we fail to comply with these guidelines, we shorten the length and quality of service we will experience. And we know that we must operate our vehicles within certain safety and care parameters to avoid damage and to maintain the best possible appearance for our vehicles, both inside and out.

Unfortunately, much of the time we don't carry this commonsense approach over into the way we care for our bodies. Because of the body's amazing ability to adjust and adapt, we think we can compromise the type of fuel we feed it, neglect periods of maintenance, and ignore reasonable operating procedures, all without serious consequences. Over many years of speaking to groups around the world about the wonder and care of the human body, I'm convinced that we don't lack knowledge of what to do; instead, we lack the will power and motivation to live according to the knowledge we already have. So, let's take a look at the complexity and creative genius of the human body to inspire a fresh commitment to honor and nurture these hidden treasures.

You truly are "fearfully and wonderfully made." Your body currently houses approximately one hundred trillion cells. Each cell has been given one trillion bits of information (the blueprint for your entire body—the DNA) and knows the specific role it has to play. The intelligence of each cell, if it were written out in English, would fill two thousand books, with each book having two thousand pages and each page containing two thousand words. You truly have been given a great treasure in your body!

Your digestive system is a wonderfully coordinated symphony of chemical and mechanical reactions designed to convert the food we eat into the raw materials for health and healing. Digestion begins when you smell mom's cooking in the kitchen, resulting in the production of saliva, a mixture of water and digestive enzymes. (Your salivary glands can produce approximately one and a half quarts of saliva every day.) Chewing is next, grinding the food into smaller pieces and blending in saliva in preparation for its journey toward your stomach.

Next, food is passed from the mouth into the esophagus and then into the stomach as small balls of material through a serious of muscular contractions. In the stomach, this food is mixed with hydrochloric acid and more digestive enzymes. Hydrochloric acid is so strong it will eat through wood, and this acidity is critical to turning your food into a liquid form before its assimilation into your body. Your stomach is protected from this potent acid by a mucous lining, except in the case of ulcers, when a portion of the mucous lining has been destroyed.

If your stomach is successful in its task, the partially digested food passes out of your stomach into the first eight to ten inches of the small intestine, called the duodenum, in a liquid form called chyme. As the chyme enters the duodenum, it mixes with bile from the liver and pancreatic enzymes that convert it from an acidic to alkaline material, making it ready for absorption into the rest of the body. This is critical to your health because your blood, which transports many of the nutrients, must remain in a relatively narrow range of alkaline pH.

Your small intestine is more than twenty feet long. Once the liquid nutrients have been alkalized in the duodenum, the material then moves over three hundred and sixty yards of surface area where small, finger-like projections called villi and microvilli dance back and forth, reaching out for nutrients to absorb into the delivery systems that transport the nutrients to the rest of your body. Lacteals, small lymphatic vessels in the villi, capture the lipids or fatty acids (fats) that will protect individual cells from damage and unwanted invaders. Capillaries in the villi transport sugars (from carbohydrates) and amino acids (from proteins) that will create energy and provide building materials for new cells and tissues.

As the liquid nutrients move through the twenty feet of small intestine into the large intestine, valuable minerals and the remaining water are absorbed into your body through the first section of the large intestine, called the ascending colon. The large intestine then moves horizontally across the center of our body (the transverse colon), meeting a variety of bacterium, whose job it is to convert the remaining waste material back into an acid material, compacting and solidifying it in preparation for removal. This is another critical chemical conversion, because lingering alkaline material in the large intestine is believed to create a breeding ground for colon cancer. Finally, turning down the descending colon, this waste material is removed from your body through another series of muscular contractions, called peristaltic action.

The digestive system works well, as long as we eat properly. This means the proper balance of dietary fibers, fats, proteins, and carbohydrates. The problem is that most people *don't* eat a balanced diet; in fact, most of us tend to eat the wrong foods altogether. Due to our harried lifestyle and the availability of quick and easy foods, the typical Western diet consists of large amounts of sugar, heavy starches, high-fat and low-fiber foods, caffeinated drinks, and alcohol. Another reason we have digestive problems is that even when we're eating the right foods, we often don't chew our food properly. We should be chewing each bite twenty-five to thirty times before swallowing. When we don't, that means our teeth haven't broken down the food sufficiently, and that puts an added stress on the rest of the digestive system. A third reason that we have digestive problems is because of the decreasing amounts of digestive juices and enzymes in our system from many years of eating too much meat and cooked food, and particularly eating microwaved food. When we microwave our food, we turn it into a toxic substance by altering the molecular form of the food (damaging the vitamin and enzyme vitality as well as creating free radicals), which puts an added strain on our digestive system. Finally, we suffer problems in our digestive system because of physical, mental, and emotional stresses, which disrupt our body's normal rhythms and create, among other problems, a lazy colon.

This adds up to a digestive system that isn't working like it should—and this creates problems. Digestive problems have become the number one reason for hospitalization in North America, and I suspect this is true in the entire industrialized world. One hundred million people in the United States suffer from digestive problems, creating a health care cost of more than $100 billion a year. Two hundred thousand Americans miss work each day because of digestive ailments!

Here are some of the most common digestive problems:

- Acid indigestion affects many people in the United States—why else do you see so many antacid commercials on TV? North Americans spend some $1 billion each year on over-the-counter antacids.

- A hiatal hernia is an abnormal protrusion of the top of the stomach through the diaphragm and into the chest cavity. The result is that the acidic juices in the stomach flow back up into the esophagus, resulting in severe heartburn.

- Diarrhea costs North Americans about $120 million in over-the-counter medications each year. Diarrhea is very uncomfortable, causes disruption in a busy schedule, and can become life-threatening because of the resulting dehydration. Recurring diarrhea is a significant way the digestive system tells us there is something wrong. Unfortunately, most of our money and effort is expended mitigating the symptoms of diarrhea rather than identifying and eliminating the cause.

• Irritable Bowel Syndrome affects ten to fifteen percent of all adults, and is second only to the common cold as a reason for a visit to the doctor's office. It is also referred to as a spastic colon and its symptoms include abdominal pain, distension, constipation, diarrhea, nausea, and heartburn.

• Diverticulitus and diverticulosis are conditions involving small protrusions, or balloons, in the large intestine or colon. In diverticulosis, these small balloons or pockets are formed through a weakening of the colon. With diverticulitis, the pockets become infected and extremely painful, resulting in nausea, vomiting, chills, and fever.

• A prolapsed colon occurs when the transverse colon, running across the front of the abdomen, falls from its normal position because of accumulated fecal matter and rests on other organs of the body, causing discomfort and potential inflammation to the other organs. Some researchers have hypothesized this is a major cause of complications in female reproductive organs as well as other internal problems.

• Colitis is an inflammation of the large intestine, which results in excruciating pain and is often accompanied with recurrent diarrhea. Other symptoms of this condition include a feeling of weakness through the abdomen, headaches, dizziness, emaciation, and pains in other parts of the body. In severe cases of colitis, there may be severe abdominal cramps, bleeding from the rectum, and fever.

• Parasite infestation is much more common than many people realize. Parasites can be transferred through unclean food, water, and household pets and include many types—some that can cause various temporary illnesses and others that can be dangerous, even deadly.

- Obstruction of the colon can happen with a build up of fecal matter due to incomplete eliminations. This creates discomfort and becomes a breeding ground for disease.

- Lazy Bowel Syndrome, or atrophy of the large intestine, often leads to a dependence on unhealthy chemical laxatives. The bowel loses its peristaltic tone, much the way a muscle loses its strength through lack of exercise. As a result, when the colon should be eliminating toxic waste material, it cannot rouse up the necessary muscular contractions for thorough evacuation, leaving waste material behind to ferment and putrefy in the colon.

- Colon cancer has become the second-leading cancer killer in North America, with more than one hundred fifty thousand new cases each year and some sixty thousand deaths. Colon cancer is thought to be caused, or at least significantly promoted, by the interaction between bacteria in the colon and a high-fat, low-fiber diet, which is exactly what most Western societies consume.

- Constipation—who hasn't suffered from this condition? More than five million people in North America see a doctor each year for constipation and spend $1 billion for prescription and over-the-counter laxatives. We should have two or three bowel movements each day, well-formed "floaters" about twelve to eighteen inches long, with little or no smell. Constipation may be more than just a health problem by itself. Dr. Denis Burkitt, one of the pioneers in research of fiber and digestion, has noted that constipation may be the cause of varicose veins, hemorrhoids, diverticular disease, and hiatal hernias. And the saddest thing about this is that constipation is easy to beat, largely through diet.

- Toxic colon. Just like dirt builds up in homes, so toxins build up in our bodies. Our environment is full of pollutants, and our food is full of additives. In addition, our body is a walking chemical factory that produces as many as ten thousand different chemicals, mostly based on the quality of the raw materials we provide to it through our diet. When we eat a healthful diet of fruits, vegetables, whole grains, and legumes, our body produces chemicals that enhance the functioning of the rest of our body. But when we eat junk food, high amounts of animal fats and proteins, sugars, and white flour, and add coffee, soft drinks, and various dairy products, our chemical factories have no choice but to do the best they can with the raw materials we give them. All of this adds up to toxicity. Government estimates indicate that we consume an average of eight to fifteen pounds of harmful chemicals each year. The combination of poor food choices and increasing intake of harmful chemicals often results in a build-up of fecal matter and mucus in the colon, sort of a papier-mâché crust. The average adult colon should weigh two to three pounds, but in reality the average colon weighs between ten to fifteen pounds. And in some autopsies researchers have found colons that weigh up to sixty pounds! That added weight is accumulated, fermented, decaying fecal matter that can be extremely toxic and a breeding ground for disease. And this can even be true for people who have a bowel movement every day. Furthermore, if your digestive tract is encrusted, nutrients can't be absorbed as well, which may lead to other health problems. So, the environmental toxins and the bad food we eat build up in the colon, and we become toxic to our own body. This can result in digestive pain, gas, bloating, skin problems, fatigue, parasite infestation, and much more.

So what can you do about these problems? Solutions include

lifestyle practices that are simple and easy to do every day, and others that will take a little more effort, depending on the severity of the condition.

- First and foremost is to decrease or eliminate bad foods from your diet by replacing them with more fruits and vegetables and whole grains. Start by reducing your sugar intake, the amount of white flour from breads and rolls, overly processed or cooked foods, and meat.

- Second, you can increase the amount of fiber in your diet to at least thirty grams per day. Today the average person only eats around twelve grams of fiber daily. A diet that includes seventy to eighty percent fruits and vegetables, with the balance consisting of whole grains and legumes, is one of the best ways to achieve this level of fiber in your diet. Fiber is extremely important in digestive health. In general terms, dietary fiber is residue from plant foods that is resistive to breakdown by digestive enzymes in the mouth, stomach, and small intestine, so it passes into the large intestine or colon. One of fiber's more important roles is to clean out, or "sweep" the digestive system. Rather than letting waste materials linger in your digestive system for long periods of time, fiber helps this material be eliminated as quickly and efficiently as possible. Most of the "processed" foods available today are devoid of fiber, including most breads and white rice, which have had the fiber completely stripped away. And, of course, animal products contain no fiber at all.

- Third, you can increase the water intake in your diet to eight to ten glasses per day, spread throughout the day, so your body has fresh water to use when it needs it. And the best water to drink is either distilled or purified by a reverse osmosis water filter. Considering that you are made up of approximately seventy percent water, it is amazing how much you can improve your sense of well-being by just getting

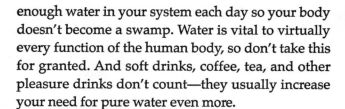

enough water in your system each day so your body doesn't become a swamp. Water is vital to virtually every function of the human body, so don't take this for granted. And soft drinks, coffee, tea, and other pleasure drinks don't count—they usually increase your need for pure water even more.

- Fourth, you can make moderate and regular exercise a regular part of your lifestyle. Exercise plays an important role in the body's cleansing process, both by stimulating the lymphatic system and by stimulating peristaltic action in the colon.

- Fifth, you can supplement your diet with herbs, fiber, and friendly bacteria—and don't use chemical laxatives to keep yourself regular. They are habit forming and can damage your liver at the same time. Instead, find natural ways to supplement your diet, with herbs and fiber and friendly bacteria, such as lactobacillus salivarius and lactobacillus acidophilus.

The first five suggestions apply to everyone. In addition, here are some more aggressive suggestions for those with chronic digestive problems.

- Sixth, you can go on a cleansing diet or a fast. Before you do this, you should either be well educated about the various factors related to fasting, or be under the care of a qualified health practitioner. Unfortunately, many medical doctors have very limited knowledge about fasting and you may have to search for a well-informed practitioner. Detoxification is recommended by many natural health practitioners to get rid of waste buildup in the body, and there are several good books available on this subject.

- Seventh, for severe digestive problems, you should seek the services of a qualified colon hydrotherapist who can help you restore a healthy condition in your digestive tract. Colon hydrotherapy is a specialized practice of restoring health to the colon through a series of colonic treatments where water is used to cleanse and tone the colon. Once again, be sure to work with a qualified, trained practitioner.

If you'd like more information about better colon health, there are quite a few terrific books on the subject. I recommend Dr. Norman Walker's book, *Colon Health: The Key to a Vibrant Life*. It's packed with valuable information about how you can take better care of your digestive system.

Action Steps

1. Make a list of everything you eat for the next week, categorizing foods into "good" and "bad" columns. Strive to create a lifestyle where at least eighty percent of your intake is foods that you know are good, providing the highest possible "octane" fuel for your body.

2. Keep a log of your bowel movements for a week, recording frequency, ease of elimination, bulk, and length of material, recognizing that this information provides significant data about your digestive health.

3. Set aside a three-day period to go on a liquid fast (no solid foods) to give your digestive system a vacation. Though *I don't recommend it to anyone without proper training,* my wife and I have enjoyed several liquid fasts as long as forty days with excellent results to our overall health.

For more information about digestive health, visit www.lifequestintl.com.

Points to Ponder

"Of the 22,000 operations I personally performed I never found a single normal colon, and of the 100,000 performed under my jurisdiction not over 6% were normal." — Harvey W. Kellogg,

M.D. (of the Kellogg family, manufacturers of breakfast cereals)

"The kind and quality of the food you put into your body is of vital importance to every phase of your existence. Good nutrition regenerates and rebuilds the cells and tissues which constitute your physical body. The elimination of undigested food and other waste products is equally as important. In simple words, the colon is the sewage system of the body. Nature's laws of preservation and hygiene require and insist that this sewage system be cleansed regularly, under penalty of the innumerable ailments, sicknesses and diseases that follow, as night follows day." — Norman Walker, D.SC, Ph.D., from *Colon Health: The Key to a Vibrant Life*

"The all-American diet that relies on processed foods—frozen foods, canned foods, convenience foods, which have been prepared from modified food materials low in fiber and many nutrients—causes the bowel contents to move slowly, to stagnate and collect on the colon wall, to become entrapped in mucus. These food and waste particles coat and clog the microvilli and become packed, sometimes as hard as concrete. Nutrients cannot be passed to the blood to feed the body's cells. Cellular waste cannot be passed to the bowel for elimination. The body attempts to eliminate the cellular waste via the kidneys, lungs, skin and sinuses. We may think modern conveniences, money and material things are important, until we lose our health. Then we would give up all we have to regain it, but our health cannot be bought. It is something that must be nourished through the years." — Teresa Schumacher & Toni Lund, *Cleansing the Body and the Colon for a Happier and Healthier You*

Chapter 18
The Circulatory System

It's a delivery service, a trash collector, a chemical manufacturer, a paramedic, a military defense, and a thermostat all working simultaneously to support seventy-five trillion customers who demand service twenty-four hours a day. This, in a nutshell, is your circulatory system—a vast army of microscopic workers that provide the continuous flow of services and supplies you need for survival.

As an adult, you have twenty-five trillion red blood cells traveling through one hundred thousand miles of veins and arteries to deliver oxygen to seventy-five trillion cells throughout your body. Having delivered their cargo, the red blood cells collect carbon dioxide (trash) that will be removed through respiration. Three thousand of these red blood cells could be placed side by side in a space shorter than an inch. Two to three million red blood cells are created in your bone marrow *every second*. These replace the two to three million that complete their life-giving mission and die every second. In some spaces, your capillaries are so small (thinner than a human hair) that these red blood cells must line up single file and squeeze themselves in odd shapes in order to deliver their cargo to the end users. Packed inside each microscopic red blood cell are more than two hundred million molecules of hemoglobin. This is what enables the red blood cell to carry and deliver oxygen.

You also have billions of white blood cells that are the defenders of your body, the mechanism by which you repel unwanted invaders that carry disease and infections. These white blood cells, assigned by the immune system, surround and encapsulate an invader and then absorb it into their own protoplasm, often sacrificing themselves in the process. There are several kinds of defenders, with the largest forces made up of neutrophils, lymphocytes, and monocytes. These soldiers are also manufactured in your bone marrow, with some of them getting additional specialized training later in your thymus after gathering particular intelligence about the enemy—but more about that later.

In addition, your circulatory system transports tens of billions of platelets, disk-like structures that prevent a loss of blood from damaged vessels. They rush to the scene of injury to apply immediate first aid and stop the loss of blood by piling up on top of each other and releasing substances that begin the process of blood clotting. Without them, the slightest injury to a vessel would result in death.

All of these amazing workers are transported to their place of work by plasma, the liquid portion of your blood. Plasma is ninety percent water, with the remaining ten percent an assortment of solids that include amino acids, minerals, vitamins, lipids, glucose, and proteins, including enzymes. Plasma also transports waste materials such as urea, uric and lactic acid, and creatinine to waste treatment facilities such as your lungs, kidneys, spleen and liver. It delivers hormones from one part of the body to another as well.

The energy source for this transportation system is your heart, a muscle about the size of an adult's fist that weighs less than one pound. In a typical day, the heart contracts one hundred thousand times, delivering enough blood to fill a four thousand-gallon tank. It processes a complete cycle of the circulatory system, running blood through the entire one hundred thousand miles of veins and arteries every minute. The work it performs each day is equivalent to lifting one hundred pounds off the ground fifteen hundred times. And it performs this function twenty-four hours a day, seven days per week, three hundred sixty-five days per year, for an average lifespan of around eighty years. That means the typical heart repeats its function 2.9 billion times with no more rest than what it grabs in between contractions. It truly is "awesome" to recognize the treasure of your circulatory system.

And yet, one American dies every forty-five seconds from a disease of the circulatory system. Cardiovascular disease is the number-one killer in the Western world today. For forty percent of the people who die from heart attacks, sudden death is the first symptom. Research shows that most people already have advanced stages of cardiovascular disease in their early twenties, though diagnosis will not come for most of them until their fifties and sixties.

The most common form of cardiovascular disease is arteriosclerosis, which is a hardening of the arteries. Deposits of oxidized fats and calcium narrow the arteries and roughen their normally smooth lining. This reduces the flow of the blood supply and, in many instances, results in blood clots. When these clots, or blockages, occur in the brain, a stroke results. When they occur in a coronary artery, they cause a heart attack. Though there is some indication that cardiovascular disease can be a result of hereditary factors, far more evidence points to habits and environment as the primary culprit for disease and premature death. Most of us don't take cardiovascular disease seriously because we don't feel any symptoms during the long years that the disease insidiously and slowly attacks our circulatory system.

Modern science can teach you much about how to protect and support the hidden treasures found within your circulatory system. As you probably know, maintaining an ideal weight plays a major role in reducing the workload on your heart. But did you know that a single pound of body fat contains almost two hundred miles of additional arteries and veins that must be serviced? Unfortunately, if you love food more than you love your body, you commit assault on your circulatory system. It's easy to make excuses for being overweight—I have a slow metabolism, it's hereditary, it's an inevitable part of aging— but science has demonstrated convincingly that "we have met the enemy and the enemy is us." Admittedly, overeating and obesity can be a complex issue involving both psychological and physiological addictions and deficiencies. It is a worthy opponent—but you must overcome it or it will steal the hidden treasures of your body.

Another way to serve your circulatory system is to reduce the quantity and improve the quality of fat in your diet. Fats found in processed and packaged foods are almost always damaging to your cardiovascular system. You should limit your dietary fat intake to somewhere between twenty and thirty percent of your total calories. Read labels and become more aware of the amount of fat as well as other non-healthful ingredients such as high amounts of sugar, processed (denatured) flours, and trans-fatty acids, like partially hydrogenated oils, including margarine. Consume the healthy fats that are found in olive oil (extra-virgin olive oil from a can is best), canola oil, and flaxseed oils as often as possible. These oils provide good raw materials for the appropriate use of fats throughout your body and are less susceptible to oxidation from the presence of free radicals (errant oxygen molecules) in your body. Increasing your intake of antioxidants, both in natural foods and supplements, also adds to the arsenal of your circulatory system in waging the war against infection and disease.

If you smoke, you can decrease your chance of suffering a heart attack by two-thirds in a relatively short period of time just by quitting. Once again, if you love your cigarettes more than you love your body, it is time to rethink the real treasures in your life.

Aerobic exercise will improve the efficiency of your circulatory system by increasing the levels of oxygen delivered throughout your body. Aerobic exercise also increases your heart rate for specific periods of time, which improves the strength and flow of energy to the heart muscle. There are specific target rates to aim for based on your age, gender, and other health considerations. Walking, jogging, swimming, biking, and playing any sport that requires consistent movement are all types of exercise that provide aerobic benefits. A qualified fitness instructor can help you develop a program that will strengthen your heart and improve the commute back and forth for all the workers in your circulatory system.

Finally, developing effective methods for managing and reducing stress also will have a direct impact on the well-being of your circulatory system. Rest, laughter, and stress decompressing all lessen the burdens on your heart muscle by improving the efficiency of each contraction, thus reducing the number of contractions required each minute. Small improvements extrapolate into significant benefits over a lifetime.

Throughout your life you will be bombarded with temptations to put other things ahead of your physical well-being. Appetites, passions, ambitions, and pretensions all call for you to serve them, often at the expense of your own long-term health. By recognizing these dangers and gaining a new reverence for the treasures within, you can rise above these enemies and realize the full value of your physical wealth.

Action Steps

1. Go through your pantry and read all the labels on your packaged foods. Every time you find a substance you shouldn't eat, such as high amounts of fat, sugar, or partially hydrogenated oil, say out loud, "Should I love this food or my body, because I cannot love them both." Then proceed as your heart tells you.

2. If you aren't already exercising every day, develop a consistent, realistic exercise program with the help of a fitness expert (either from a book or through a local fitness club). Create an exercise program that will be fun so that you will stick with it for the rest of your life.

3. Journal about your current weight and what is within your power to do to maintain your ideal weight and aerobic fitness. Find a friend you can be mutually accountable with to improve your cardiovascular health.

Points to Ponder

"One should eat to live, not live to eat." — Moliere, French playwright

"Nearly one million Americans die annually from heart disease. On the surface this might not appear so shocking, unless we know how these figures compare with those at the turn of this century [1900]. There were very few deaths from heart disease then. Why have we gone from just a few people dying annually from heart disease, to nearly one million? The answer is not simple, but it definitely involves changes in our eating habits." — Dr. Mary Ruth Swope, nutrition educator and retired dean of the School of Home Economics, Eastern Illinois University, *The Green Leaves of Barley*

Chapter 19
The Nervous System

It is your command and control system. It processes more data in an instant than a personal computer could process in ten years of constant operation. It constantly collects, analyzes, and interprets data from the environment around you and sends out new orders to the rest of your body based on its instantaneous analysis. The remarkable nervous system is made up of your brain, your spinal cord, and more than three trillion nerve cells that, lined up, would stretch some forty-five miles in length.

The nervous system contains three subsystems: the central system, the peripheral system, and the autonomic system. The central system is composed of the brain and spinal cord. It is the central switchboard and, in most cases, the decision-making component that directs the rest of your body's responses. The peripheral system is made up of twelve pairs of nerves that originate in your brain, along with thirty-one pairs of nerves that reside in your spinal column. These provide the major information transmission highways between your brain and the rest of your body. Last, the autonomic system is your auto pilot that regulates things like breathing, your heartbeat, and your digestion. This subsystem is made up of the sympathetic nervous system, which responds to special needs and emergencies, and the parasympathetic system, which normalizes functions (balancing the sympathetic system so you aren't always in crisis mode).

Nerve impulses travel up to three hundred miles per hour, processing one hundred million electrochemical impulses each second. The eye, one of several organs used for collecting data, is a fully automatic, self-focusing, non-blurring, motion picture camera that takes instant high-resolution, three-dimensional, color pictures. With one hundred twenty million photoreceptors, your eye perceives more than one million simultaneous impressions and discriminates among nearly ten million varieties in color. Your skin has approximately four million sensory structures that convey information to your brain about a variety of conditions, including touch and temperature. Similarly complex systems for data collection exist in your ears, nose, and tongue to provide research to the brain.

Your brain, which grows to three pounds by your sixth year and remains the same size through adulthood, is made up of thirty billion neurons and as many as ten times more connective cells to receive and analyze the information that travels down your nervous system's superhighway. Each of the thirty billion neurons is connected with as many as sixty thousand other neurons, creating a communication network without parallel. Though your brain represents only two percent of your total body weight, it uses twenty percent of your body's need for oxygen. It is part computer, part electrical power plant, and part chemical factory as it performs billions of tasks each day. It receives sensory messages, controls movement, regulates body processes, develops and communicates language, captures memory, processes logic, and creates emotion. It produces a variety of chemicals that are used as neurotransmitters that function in the regulation of emotions and complex movements.

There are two primary risks to the nervous system: injury and disease. Injuries include blows to the head or spinal column as well as physical trauma that results in pinched or blocked nerves. (In chiropractic medicine these are referred to as subluxations when they occur in the spinal column.) Diseases of the nervous system include infections and imbalance of the chemicals necessary for positive mental health. Stroke is the most common serious disorder of the brain; it is caused when the blood supply to the brain is cut off, resulting in the death of nerve cells due to a lack of oxygen. Tumors also can cause severe damage, either by destroying brain cells or by creating pressure in the brain that interferes with normal function. Many headaches are the result of mild viruses attacking the brain, while more serious infections, such as encephalitis or meningitis, can be lethal or cause paralysis by disconnecting certain brain functions.

Chiropractic care has provided one of the most dynamic improvements to the nervous system of the last one hundred years. I must confess that I was very skeptical of chiropractic treatment for many years. However, when I stepped out from under my cynicism and studied the basis for and results of chiropractic care, I realized it provides a non-invasive way to care for and protect the treasures of the human nervous system. Furthermore, because the nervous system is the communication and control system for every other system in your body, chiropractic care will probably improve your health in every other area also. Having said that, I don't relegate a visit to my chiropractor to those times when I can't get rid of a backache. To do this is to use chiropractic care as a way to treat symptoms, which, though it is beneficial, fails to recognize the value of promoting wellness and preventing problems before they occur. So, for many years I have made a monthly visit to my chiropractor regardless of the pain or lack thereof in my back, neck, or head.

Research over the last twenty years reveals that diet has an impact on brain function. Because the brain requires disproportionate amounts of energy, the quality of fuels (nutrients) and the ease of delivery (circulation) play an important role in nervous system health. Herbal extracts, such as garlic, ginkgo biloba, chamomile, passion flower, and valerian root, as well as minerals such as magnesium citrate and the B-complex vitamins, deliver special nutrients to the nervous system that assist in a variety of functions. As with all body systems, high-quality foods provide high-quality nutrients that support optimal performance by the nervous system, while low-quality foods compromise and stress the nervous system's ability to function properly. Your body has an amazing ability to adapt to whatever you give it. However, every compromise weakens your effectiveness and, ultimately, shortens the length of service you will enjoy from your body's hidden treasures.

Action Steps

1. Make a recurring appointment to visit a chiropractor at least once a month, regardless of any symptoms you may or may not experience.

2. Include a B-complex vitamin supplement or generous portions of foods containing high amounts of B-complex vitamins (beans, eggs, fish) in your daily diet.

3. Supplement your diet with three hundred to one thousand milligrams of magnesium citrate per day (loose bowels are an indication of magnesium saturation so if this occurs, decrease your magnesium intake just below the point that this occurs.)

Points to Ponder

"For more than one hundred years, chiropractic care has been built on a unique philosophy that recognizes living organisms as possessing a profound, inborn drive toward health and that has as its goal unleashing the body's ability to fully express its inborn potential." — Michael Lenarz, D.C., *The Chiropractic Way*

Chapter 20
The Glandular System

Small in stature, huge in importance—an apt description for a seemingly odd collection of internal organs that produce some of the most sophisticated and potent chemicals known to man. This seemingly random combination of mostly small (weighing less than one ounce), non-descript shapes throughout your body makes up the glandular system. The chemicals your glands produce are as common as sweat and as intricate as pineal gland hormone, which is so minute that it would take twenty million pineal glands to collect one quarter of an ounce.

Glands work in partnership with the nervous system to trigger all of the other functions in your body. The hormones they produce regulate the way your body uses food, how and when you grow, the function of sex and reproduction, the regulation of the composition of your blood, the reaction of your body to emergencies, and the control of the hormones themselves. The variety of glands and their functions are too vast to explain in this context, so let's take a look at a few of the major glands to gain a greater appreciation of the glandular system overall.

The pituitary gland weighs about one-fiftieth of an ounce and is made up of eighty-five percent water. It is located in the bottom of the brain, where it manufactures infinitesimal amounts of hormones that regulate all of the other hormonal production throughout your body. It is the executive office of the glandular system and combines its chemical messengers with the electrical transportation system of the nervous system to maintain balance throughout your body.

The thyroid gland sits across your windpipe, where it regulates your metabolism, or the rate at which energy is created throughout your body. It weighs only two-thirds of an ounce and produces only 1/100,000 of an ounce of hormones each day. An overproduction of the hormone it produces results in nervousness, weight loss, and an incredible appetite. An underproduction causes obesity and mental depression. One of the most important nutrients needed for proper thyroid functioning is iodine, which is found in sea vegetables like dulse, kelp and sea salt. (Most table salt also has iodine added, but it has proven to be a poor source of sodium, both because of the presence of chloride and the absence of other valuable minerals that should be balanced with sodium in your diet.)

The thymus gland, which is roughly the size of a pack of gum, is located between and near the top of the lungs. Though it is part of the glandular system, its most important function is as an advanced training center for the white blood cells. After being manufactured in the bone marrow, white blood cells travel through the thymus, where the hormone thymosin increases their proficiencies and then sends them off to the spleen and lymphatic system.

The adrenal glands are located on top of each kidney; they produce more than fifty different hormones, including some of your body's most potent. These hormones can be grouped into two primary categories. Your brain controls the first group of hormones, which are produced when they receive a message that there is an emergency, a physical threat, or some emotional response required immediately. These hormones (adrenalin and noradrenaline) instantly speed up your body's energy supply. Your heart rate speeds up, the blood vessels near your skin shut down (causing blushing), and digestion instantly stops. Every function of your body goes into emergency alert. The result is that your body can instantly run faster, jump higher, or lift greater weight because of the focused energy released at the command of these hormones. Once the emergency passes, the adrenal glands receive orders from the pituitary gland to stop producing these hormones.

The second group of hormones produced in the adrenals plays more of a regulatory role for a number of different body functions. These hormones regulate the metabolism of carbohydrates, protein, and fat. They monitor the mineral balance in the water throughout your body. And there are also hormones that supplement the sex hormones produced in your sex organs.

Exhausted or diseased adrenals can create a wide variety of symptoms, including anemia, muscle atrophy, nausea, vomiting, diarrhea, brittle bones, high blood pressure, allergies, and dementia. Fatigue of the adrenals occurs as a result of overconsumption of stimulants such as coffee and sugar, as well as from an all-work-and-no-play lifestyle.

If the pituitary gland represents the "executive office" for the glandular system, then the liver is its most complex production and storage facility. At three pounds it is by far the largest organ in the glandular system, lying in the upper-right part of your abdomen just above your stomach and small intestine. The roles it plays are so diverse and so complex that it has earned its own branch of medical research. It is actually a combination of several different chemical-manufacturing units all housed in one organ. These individual units are called lobules, and your liver has somewhere between fifty thousand and one hundred thousand of these manufacturing units.

The liver performs more than five hundred different functions and produces over one thousand kinds of enzymes, which serve as chemical catalysts for digestion, detoxification, and purification of the blood. It is the waste treatment facility for the blood, removing a number of different waste products, including used hormones that have completed their tasks. It plays a significant role in preparing macronutrients for absorption into your blood stream and provides your body's largest storage facility for a number of important vitamins, including A, D, E, K, and B12. At any given time, one quarter of your total blood supply is being processed by your liver.

The liver secretes several substances into the small intestine: bile for digestion; various blood proteins that prevent blood plasma from seeping through the walls of your blood vessels; globulins that help you fight infections; fibrinogen that helps in clotting; and cholesterol that is used to build cell membranes and manufacture other hormones. It is an awesome demonstration of how we have been "fearfully and wonderfully made."

Your glandular system gets the raw materials to perform its delicate work from your diet. Its workload is increased or decreased by your lifestyle and the environment around you. Therefore, you play a very important role in the health, life expectancy and effectiveness of this system. In *Raw Vegetable Juices*, Norman Walker writes,

> The least we can do to help our wonderful glandular system to function at its highest state of efficiency is to keep our body thoroughly cleansed of waste and corrupt matter, to nourish the body with the best natural raw foods and juices available, and learn to completely control our mind and emotions.

You add stress to your glandular system when you consume stimulants (caffeine, excessive sugar, nicotine, pharmaceuticals) and when you consume depressants (alcohol, sleeping pills, other pharmaceuticals). Consuming these substances forces a very delicate system to spend its energy restoring balance to your body. You also can stress your glandular system emotionally by living in constant conflict or not taking adequate times for rest (especially after demanding projects or particularly stressful periods in your life). Many pharmaceuticals and over-the-counter drugs or supplements seek to manipulate the glandular system. Examples of this manipulation include stimulant drugs to fight depression, depressants to fight hyperactivity or to induce sleep, and synthetic hormones that are used in birth control and for menopause (hormone replacement therapy) or to treat prostate conditions. Though these medications and supplements have helped people with severe conditions, they carry much higher risks for side affects than traditional foods and vitamin/ mineral supplements. Even those prescribed by medical professionals present significant risk and should be used only as a last resort in correcting a serious glandular problem. Recent research confirms that the continuous use of hormone therapies contributes long-term health risks and should be avoided whenever possible.

The glandular system is another remarkable hidden treasure that, when cared for properly, will help provide you with many years of good health.

Action Steps

1. Make a food journal to record everything you eat for a week (or a month), dividing each food into column one (fresh and raw) and column two (cooked, refined, or packaged). Try to have eighty percent of your foods fit into column one and only twenty percent of your foods in column two.

2. Drink two glasses of vegetable juices every day (either separate or combinations of greens, carrots, and red beets).

3. Set aside one day every week to learn how to achieve maximum rest (no work, no TV, nothing that is a food, beverage, or emotional stimulant).

For more information on vegetable juices and a protocol for a self-managed liver cleanse, visit www.lifequestintl.com.

Points to Ponder

"Disease is often a late manifestation of a process that has its origin long before symptoms developed. This is certainly true of coronary heart disease, osteoporosis, breast and other cancers, fibroids, hypertension, arthritis, and many, many others. Mainstream medicine focuses on the disease as it becomes symptomatic, not on the initial asymptomatic stages. If we are to make any advance in health care, it will come as a result of understanding initial causes, not in waiting to treat the later symptomatic phase. We stand at the confluence of profound changes. Our present medical system is symptom-fixated and driven by misplaced economic incentives, but it now faces still competition from alternative practitioners." – John R. Lee, M.D. from *What Your Doctor May Not Tell You About Menopause*

"My advice is to live your life. Allow that wonderful inner intelligence to speak through you. The blueprint for you to be your authentic self lies within. In some mystical way the microscopic egg that grew to be you had the program for your physical, intellectual, emotional and spiritual development. Allow the development to occur to its fullest; grow and bloom."
Bernie S. Siegel, M.D. from *Love, Medicine & Miracles*

Chapter 21
The Respiratory System

What do you suppose the most important nutrient is for your health and well-being? You can live for at least forty days without food. You can live for three or more days without water, depending on the environment around you. But how long can you live without oxygen? Only minutes.

Your respiratory system is one of the simplest systems in your body. You breathe in air through your nose and mouth, it is deposited in your lungs, where a small portion of the oxygen molecules are picked up in your blood, and you exhale some carbon dioxide to complete the process of external respiration. All of this happens automatically, for the most part, without thought or effort. However, beneath the surface another miracle of the human body is taking place.

Most of us think of our lungs like balloons, inflating when we breathe in and deflating when we breathe out. In reality, the lungs are more like large sponges, filled with hundreds of millions of "loading docks" packing their valuable cargo for delivery to the one hundred trillion cells throughout your body. As air passes through your nose, mouth, and windpipe, it is conditioned in preparation for introduction into the lungs. The air must be warmed, moistened, and filtered. Surprisingly, the lungs are fairly passive in the process of inhalation and exhalation. The exchange of air takes place through a combination of contractions in the chest and diaphragm, along with a slightly lower atmospheric pressure inside the chest cavity, which results in a vacuum that sucks air into the lungs when your muscles contract and releases air when your muscles relax. But the lungs don't play an active role in the exchange of gases.

As the conditioned air makes its way into your lungs, it passes through smaller and smaller branches. First, it passes through the bronchial tubes, then the smaller bronchioles, which are only one-one hundredth of an inch thick. Finally, the air arrives in the alveoli, or the "loading zone," where red blood cells line up single-file through tiny capillaries. This close partnership between the cardiovascular and respiratory systems allows the oxygen molecules, which are abundant in your lungs, to jump across single-cell walls of the capillaries, where they are quickly attracted to the hemoglobin in the red blood cells. This vital cargo is then shipped throughout your body by the contracting of your heart. As the red blood cells reach their destinations, the oxygen molecules jump off and provide a valuable component in the production of cellular energy by performing a leading role in the Krebs cycle, which is a series of chemical reactions that creates energy. As a result of the Krebs cycle and a second series of reactions called the electron transport chain, carbon dioxide and water are formed as waste products and the final product, energy, is stored as ATP (adenosine triphosphate) in your cells for later use. The red blood cells pick up the carbon dioxide and bring it back to the lungs, where it jumps back into one of the hundreds of millions of alveoli and is exhaled out of your nose or mouth.

In reality, respiration isn't all that efficient. The air you breathe is almost twenty-one percent oxygen, with the vast majority of the remaining molecules being nitrogen. Yet you capture only about twenty percent of the oxygen you inhale, so that you exhale eighty percent of the oxygen you took in. And when you exhale, five percent of the air leaving your lungs is made up of carbon dioxide. So, you still exhale more than three times more oxygen than carbon dioxide.

Why, in light of the remarkable efficiencies of your other body systems, is the respiratory system so "inefficient"? Maybe it is a defense mechanism, since you have so little control over the air you breathe. This system protects you from the wide, often unnoticed, variances in the air you breathe. Dust, smoke, and other pollutants are constantly being drawn into the lungs with little or no recognition. By using only a small portion of the available oxygen, the lungs are able to effectively minimize or eliminate the invasion of harmful substances into the blood stream.

Your lungs are capable of holding up to eight pints of air, yet during each breath you draw in about only one pint. While you are lying still, you need about eight pints of air per minute. If you are working at a desk, you need about sixteen pints per minute. Walking requires twenty-four pints per minute, and a fast run can require up to fifty pints per minute. Contrary to popular belief, aerobic exercise doesn't literally increase your lung capacity. Instead, it increases the muscular strength of your chest muscles and diaphragm, which engages more of the lung capacity that already exists.

Like almost all other regulatory systems, the brain triggers the regulation of your breathing. Your brain has chemical gauges that constantly measure the levels of carbon dioxide in your blood stream. As the levels rise, your brain sends orders to your muscles to involuntarily contract and draw in more air, and your heart keeps the new supplies of oxygen moving throughout your body. This regulatory system can be overridden, either through hormonal releases such as adrenalin (speeding up the process), or through a conscious effort to hold your breath (slowing down the process). However, the automatic respiratory system will force you to begin breathing again before you faint from elevated levels of carbon dioxide.

How can you tap into this hidden treasure for greater results? First, by increasing your breathing capacity and second, by becoming more conscious of, and proactive about, the quality of the air you breathe. You can increase your capacity through aerobic exercise, which increases your rate of breathing and heart rate within a safe range. In addition, you can increase your capacity through deep breathing exercises. This is particularly important during times of increased stress. Choosing a better quality of air to breathe starts with spending time outside every day. In spite of outdoor pollution caused by automotive, agricultural, and industrial waste, indoor pollution has proven to be far more toxic and dangerous. Indoor pollutants include gases from carpets, particleboard, and a whole host of other building materials. Gas appliances, such as furnaces, ovens, and water heaters, also release pollutants that accumulate over time. So, the first thing you can do to improve the air you breathe is to take every opportunity to get outside.

In addition, there are a number of ways to purify indoor air, ranging from the placement of various green plants indoors that release oxygen and absorb pollutants, to the installation of room purifiers that remove allergens, dust, and other pollutants. One of the more misunderstood, but most effective ways to purify air, is through ozone purifiers, which release ozone (O_3) into the air to attack and neutralize pollutants. This potent form of oxygen is often confused with atmospheric pollution, which is often measured by the amount of ozone present which has attached itself to toxic particles to cleanse the fouled air.

Action Steps

1. Inhale slowly during a count to ten, and then exhale slowly during a ten count. Do this for five minutes, three times a day, breathing deeply from your belly area.

2. Spend a minimum of two hours outside every day that you can, taking some time to breathe deeply. Whenever possible, exercise outside.

3. Do at least thirty minutes of aerobic exercise at least three times each week, taking your heartbeat to your target range for at least twenty minutes each time. Your target range can be calculated by using the following formula:

> Maximum heart rate = 208 − (0.7 x age in years)
> Your training target should be 75–80% of your maximum heart rate.

> Example: 50 years old
> Maximum heart rate = 208 − (0.7 x 50) = 173
> Training target rate = 130–138 heart beats per minute

Points to Ponder

"The more oxygen you can breathe into your lungs, the more energy you will have. It is very much like a fire in a fireplace. The more oxygen the fire gets, the brighter it will burn. The less it gets, the less fire and more unwanted smoke it makes." — Patricia Bragg, Naturopathic Doctor, Ph.D., *Super Power Breathing for Super Energy*

"Learning to breathe is an essential ingredient in obtaining optimal health. Why? Because deeper, fuller breathing not only increases the physical amount of oxygen needed to drive the body's metabolic processes, but also assuages tissue spasticities and releases tension. By freeing up blocked feelings and emotions, breathing gets the body in touch with feeling. As a psychotherapist, I have seen many patients perform deep-breathing exercises and as a result experience deep feelings, crying, and emotional release. This release in itself is healing. Breathing is thus the focus of any body-oriented therapy." — Stephen T. Sinatra, M.D. from *Optimum Health*

Chapter 22
The Structural System

No robot has yet been created to duplicate what you take for granted. You write your name, bounce a basketball while running, walk up and down stairs, and pull weeds in your garden. Day after day you use a wonderful combination of bones and muscles to do ordinary things because of the inestimable treasure that is your structural system.

The structural system is made up of bones, muscles, tendons, and ligaments. It serves three important and primary functions. First, it gives shape, structure, flexibility, and mobility to all of the other treasures within. Next, it provides valuable protection to vulnerable organs. Finally, it manufactures and stores additional building materials for your life.

You have around two hundred and six bones, which are made up of twenty-one percent water, twenty-seven percent organic substances, and fifty-two percent inorganic salts. Your bones are tube-like structures that contain ninety-nine percent of the calcium in your body and more than eighty-five percent of the phosphorus. Their tubular structure makes them much stronger than if they were solid. In addition, your bones house a manufacturing facility in their hollow center, where marrow manufactures red blood cells, the oxygen transports of your bloodstream, and white blood cells, the infantrymen of your immune system. Your bones are continuously storing and releasing calcium, sodium, and phosphorus into your bloodstream, maintaining a critical balance for life. This balance allows nerves to transport their impulses throughout your body, muscles to contract, and your heart to beat.

Two significant ways you can support this exchange of minerals in your body is by refraining from drinking soft drinks and milk. Soft drinks disrupt the mineral balance in your body by flooding it with phosphoric acid, which has a chemical structure the body considers foreign. It analyzes the phosphoric acid and identifies the closest natural substance, phosphorus, which is always partnered with calcium throughout the body. Therefore, your bones start sacrificing calcium in an attempt to balance the phosphoric acid, and the result is an epidemic of osteoporosis in adults, causing porous and brittle bones. Refraining from drinking milk is a bit more controversial, in large part because of successful advertising by dairy associations. Milk does contain calcium and calcium does build strong bones. However, cow's milk contains calcium lactate, which has been rendered unusable through pasteurization. (Calcium carbonate, a popular form of calcium supplement, should also be avoided. Instead, the best source of calcium is deep-green, leafy vegetables and the juices extracted from green foods. When additional supplementation is needed, calcium citrate is the most effective form.) Milk also contains approximately three hundred percent more casein than human milk, which makes it one of the most mucus-forming substances you can ingest. Casein is a primary ingredient in manufacturing glues for wood. Over and over again, parents report that chronic ear and respiratory conditions disappear when they quit giving their children cow's milk. Of course, serious scientific studies have demonstrated that cow's milk is very nutritious—for calves, who grow from seventy-five pounds to as much as two thousand pounds during their journey to maturity.

Your bones also provide valuable protection to organs throughout your body. Your brain, obviously crucial because of its command and control functions, is protected by the thickest bone structure in your body, your skull. Your skull is made up of twenty-nine bones, including eight cranial and fourteen facial. These fit together like a jigsaw puzzle to protect your brain while providing flexibility. Your ribs protect your abdominal area, which houses your heart, lungs, kidneys, liver, stomach, and intestines. Your pelvic bones protect your reproductive and elimination organs. And your spinal column protects a vast web of nerves sending messages throughout your body.

Your bones also function as a complex combination of levers

that, when combined with the muscles, tendons, and ligaments, give you incredible flexibility and mobility. Move your arms in a large circle. Put them behind your back, over your head. Touch your feet with your hands and then put a finger on the tip of your nose. Every one of these movements is a treasure you have been given. If you disagree, ask Christopher Reeve— he will tell you how privileged you are to have a healthy structural system. Now complete each of these movements again—with awe and gratitude!

Your six hundred muscles make up forty percent of your body weight. They are connected to your bones by tendons that grab hold of your bones and don't let go, acting like strings on a puppet. They make it possible for your muscles and bones to work as one unit. Ligaments also play a role by holding everything in proper relationship while movement takes place. They protect the nerves running through your muscles, they hold the blood vessels in place, and they keep the tendons in perfect position to continue "pulling your strings." The structural muscles always work in pairs (or opposites) because the muscles can pull but not push.

Your muscles are made of various types of protein, with minerals playing a vital role— exciting them with something scientists call electric potential. Adenosine triphosphate (ATP), a substance created by oxygen and chemical reactions in your cells, provides the energy for movement. Your muscles receive commands from both nerve impulses and hormones, depending on the muscle. All of this happens with deep, complex intelligence, even if you employ your muscles with little or no thought.

Like every other physical treasure in your body, your structural system needs good raw materials to build bone, muscle, and tissue. A balanced, natural diet (as opposed to refined, packaged, and junk foods), along with plenty of water, regular exercise, and proactive stress management, will help you mine this treasure for its greatest value and length of service.

Action Steps

1. Take fifteen minutes in the morning and again in the evening to do some stretching. Don't "bounce" your muscles or stretch to a point of discomfort. Instead, use stretching to discover your flexibility once again and to slowly increase your range of motion over time. Think about what is going on in your body as you stretch.

2. Work with a trainer (either in person or via a book) to set up a weight lifting program that includes three workouts every week, with a day of rest between each workout.

3. Have at least one serving of deep green, leafy vegetables every day. Eat some raw, such as romaine lettuce, spinach, and mixed greens, and steam others, such as kale, broccoli, and beet greens, adding some extra-virgin olive oil, lemon juice, or Bragg's Aminos, available in health food stores, for flavoring.

Points to Ponder

"I just don't believe that anyone in this world sets out on a journey to become fat and unhealthy, just as no one decides to become lonely or poor. What happens is, somewhere along the line, slowly and gradually, without even being aware of it, we give up. We give up our values and our dreams one at a time. When people let go of their bodies, it is, quite simply, the beginning of the end." –Bill Phillips, *Body For Life—12 Weeks to Mental and Physical Strength*

For more articles on improving your structural system, visit www.bodybuilding.com.

Chapter 23
The Immune System

At first glance, the immune system doesn't look like a system at all. Its parts are spread all over the body and seem to work independently of each other. It includes the largest organ in the body and microscopic cells that all play a part in a never-ending war against a myriad of invaders. Yet without its vigilance, you would not live more than two days.

Much like a medieval castle, the immune system is a fortress designed to keep enemies out. Your first line of defense is the largest organ of your body, your skin. It is considered an organ because of the many activities it performs. In a one-fourth-inch square of skin, you have three feet of capillaries, ten hair follicles, fifteen oil glands, twelve feet of nerves, and one hundred sweat glands. Your skin is able to withstand cold, heat, toxins, bacteria, and viruses. It acts as both a physical and chemical barrier, preventing access to invaders (unless it is breeched by a laceration) and killing them in time because of its slightly acidic pH.

Of course, we do need some openings in our skin to breathe, eat, hear, see, smell, and talk. These provide the second avenue of attack from bacteria, viruses, pathogens, fungi, and parasites. Because you are vulnerable here, the second line of defense from the immune system is the mucous membranes in each of these openings. Upon notification that an invader has entered, these membranes produce mucus, which traps and washes away the invaders, preventing them from entering deeper into your body. When you catch a cold, the mucous membranes produce additional mucus to capture and dispose of the culprits that would otherwise threaten your survival. (So why do we take medicine to shut down this process?) When you get an allergic response, such as hay fever, the membranes are overreacting because they don't recognize the pollens that are entering your system.

Mucous membranes do what they can, but some of the invaders make it beyond their defenses and burrow their way into your blood stream. This is when the true infantrymen and special forces spring into action. The white blood cells, manufactured in your bone marrow, play a number of different roles in the war. They have a variety of capabilities based on the training they receive in the bone marrow (B cells) and advanced training in the thymus gland (T cells). B cells produce antibodies that work to eliminate pathogens. Each B cell can produce only one type of antibody, but it can produce up to five hundred thousand molecules of its special antibody to attack. Throughout the population of B cells, they are capable of making millions of different antibodies based on the assignment given to each cell. B cells are also capable of cloning themselves quickly to grow an instant army once the enemy has been identified.

T cells are the white blood cells that have attended advanced training in the thymus. There are three different kinds of T cells. Killer T cells attack and consume bacteria and viruses. Helper T cells send messages for more antibodies and direct the attack based on reconnaissance. Suppressor T cells produce a chemical that stops the attack once the victory over a pathogen has been won.

Macrophages are large scavenger cells that surround and eat up bacteria, viruses, and other unwanted debris. Neutrofils and monocytes are part of this contingency, and a special protein warrior, called complement, occasionally joins them. All of these "smart" white blood cells are able to retain a detailed memory of the invaders they fight. In some instances, they retain and pass this information on to future white blood cells for your entire lifetime. In other cases, such as common colds, they lose their memory over time and have to be retrained when the virus returns later.

In addition to this wonderful army, there are other ways your immune system is supplied. First, and most important, water plays a vital role in winning the war against invaders. Your body is made up of approximately seventy percent water. Your blood and lymph fluids are both more than ninety percent water. One of the surest ways to clear out unwanted invaders is to replace this water on a timely basis. This means drinking at least half of your body weight in ounces each day. For example, if you weigh one hundred fifty pounds, then you should drink at least seventy-five ounces of water each day. If you drink soft drinks, alcohol, or drinks containing caffeine, then you need to drink considerably more water because all of these beverages have a dehydrating effect on your body. Some scientists believe dehydration is the number one cause of disease today, primarily because of the way water cleanses. When sufficient water is ingested, the kidneys cleanse the blood by processing fifty gallons through more than forty miles of tubing each day, resulting in a mere quart of urine for the elimination of urea and uric acid. And to prevent diluting your digestive juices, you should drink your water between meals, which means a half hour before a meal or three hours after.

Exercise also has been shown to improve immune system response. Lymphatic fluids are circulated more effectively throughout your body when you exercise, especially with aerobic exercise or jumping on a trampoline. This stimulation of the lymphatic system helps to clean out pathogens and debris. Exercise also affects your attitude and production of hormones, providing additional support to your immune system.

Antioxidants also make a significant impact on immune response. One of the most commonly accepted theories of disease and aging concerns the damage cells incur when they are attacked by renegade oxygen molecules, called free radicals. These molecules are missing an electron, so they steal from others, setting off a chain reaction that scientists now believe is a primary factor in the development of almost every degenerative disease. Antioxidants help to neutralize these free radicals and, in doing so, can prevent a wide variety of degenerative diseases, including cardiovascular disease, cancer, arthritis, cataracts, and almost every condition involving inflammation. Many antioxidants are available through diet and supplementation, including vitamins A, C,

E, and B-complex, beta-carotene, the minerals potassium, selenium, copper, iron, zinc, magnesium, herbs such as garlic, ginkgo biloba extract and green tea extract, and the enzymes CoQ10, superoxide dismutase, methione reductase, catalase, and glutathione preoxidase. These antioxidants either act as scavengers to seek out and devour free radicals, or they support other substances that do.

Finally, one of the greatest ways to support the immune system is through adequate rest. When you rest, your body can marshal its resources to focus on increasing immune system activity and speed up the healing process. Benjamin Franklin wrote, "Early to bed, early to rise, keeps a man strong, healthy and wise." He intuitively understood something about your immune system that can serve you well as you continue to benefit from this hidden treasure.

Action Steps

1. Take at least one antioxidant supplement every day and include at least one antioxidant-rich oil in your diet every day (extra-virgin olive oil, flax seed oil, etc.). If you need help with deciding what to take, e-mail me at info@lifequestintl.com.

2. Before going to bed each night, take three minutes to visualize all of the emotional trash you picked up during the day, then put it in an imaginary trash can and put the can out on your imaginary street as a way of clearing your mind of the stresses of the day. (Adapted from *The Power of Positive Thinking* by Dr. Norman Vincent Peale.)

3. Figure how much water you should drink each day by dividing your weight (pounds) in half and then drinking that much water in ounces between meals.

Points to Ponder

"We should accept the responsibility for the care of our own health. Most of us desire a gratifyingly long, ailment-free life. There is no way to achieve this other than to do things that are good for our health and to avoid practices that cause our bodies to deteriorate." —Francisco Contreras, M.D. from *Health in the 21st Century*

"How does the body protect and repair itself, rejuvenate and rebuild tissues torn down through wear and tear of daily living? I believe it is done through using the same chemical elements from which it was made—minerals, vitamins, enzymes, protein, carbohydrates, fats, and water. I do not believe it is accomplished through drugs and man-made concoctions containing specific amounts and types of unnatural elements. Nothing man can put together in the way of magic formulas for health will ever heal or rebuild or promote growth like the products provided for us by nature." —Dr. Mary Ruth Swope, from *The Green Leaves of Barley*

"My research has shown that the green leaves of the embryonic barley plant contain the most prolific balanced supply of nutrients that exist on earth in a single source." — Yoshihide Hagiwara, M.D. from *Green Barley Essence*

Part IV
Diamonds of the Spirit

"Once, having been asked by the Pharisees when the kingdom of God would come, Jesus replied, 'The kingdom of God does not come with your careful observation, nor will people say, "Here it is," or "There it is," because the kingdom of God is within you.'"
— Luke 17:20–21

Chapter 24
Faith

To excavate "diamonds of the spirit" is to explore the greatest diamond mines of all. These are the treasures discovered at the deepest level of your being. They are formed through the greatest pressures and greatest heat, and they are the most difficult to discover. Yet they are also the most valuable, both because of their brilliance and their permanence. These treasures are the true authentication that "diamonds are forever."

Before digging into these quarries, I should qualify a few of my convictions about this sensitive and intimate area or your life. Diamonds of the spirit have been at the core of my existence. From an early age, spiritual hunger drove me to seek these treasures in a variety of ways. My grandfather, a Congregational minister, would take me on long walks and tell story after story about his spiritual journey and the adventure of having a relationship with God. His confidence in this relationship continues to inspire me decades later in my own search for these treasures. His faith wasn't the result of deep theological contemplation or his seminary training. If anything, these achievements were impediments to his experience rather than catalysts. Rather, the expression of his faith was the continuous pursuit of a relationship, a communion with an invisible, yet ever- present God—as a Person.

This example has helped me to avoid becoming overly intellectual in my own quest. I am regularly reminded of the words of Jesus to His disciples: "I tell you the truth, unless you change and become like little children, you will never enter the kingdom of heaven. Therefore, whoever humbles himself like this child is the greatest in the kingdom of heaven" (Matthew 18:3–4).

What did Jesus mean by this? That the attitude that leads to unearthing true spiritual treasures is one of humility and simple trust, in contrast with intellectual snobbery and pride, which seeks to impress, control, and manipulate. In this spirit, I invite you to journey with me along this path of discovery. It is interesting that Jesus' greatest conflicts always came with the religious leaders of His day. How was it that this great spiritual giant was in almost constant conflict with the religious leaders of His time? Why didn't they recognize Him for who and what He was? How could they be the offspring of so many great spiritual pioneers and traditions, yet be so blinded to the manifestation of divinity in their midst?

More important, how can we keep ourselves from becoming just like those religious leaders? Humility, childlike trust, a hunger to discover more of God, and a constant turning away from, or rejection of, pride, self-serving power, and presumption make up the compass we will need for this journey.

One more qualifier is necessary before we begin this journey. Over the years I have been privileged to work with and become friends with people from many different religious traditions. Their religious practices have never hindered my love for or appreciation of them. In fact, the differences in our convictions often have enriched my life and served as opportunities for us to deepen our friendships with one another. It has always struck me as a precious opportunity to earn enough trust with someone that he is willing to share his most sacred inner beliefs with me. Long ago, I realized that if I limited my interaction and loyalties to people who agree with me, it would be a very lonely and shallow existence (my wife and I don't even agree on everything!) Rather than being threatened by our differences, I am learning to enjoy our differences and to appreciate the passion that stirs people to search for spiritual treasures.

At the same time, I believe that there are diamonds and there are zircons in the quest for spiritual treasures. A zircon may look like a diamond to the untrained eye, and for many people it is enough. But it still isn't a diamond—it exhibits the form

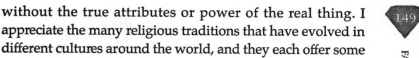

without the true attributes or power of the real thing. I appreciate the many religious traditions that have evolved in different cultures around the world, and they each offer some degree of truth, beauty, and purpose. However, I also believe in eternal treasures that are not the product of religious tradition. They are the substance upon which the religious traditions have come into being. We might say that religious traditions are merely shadows or remembrances of real treasures, and for many people, this is the closest they will ever get to the real thing. After more than thirty years of study and adventure, it is my conviction that the eternal, spiritual treasures are personified and revealed in the Person of Jesus of Nazareth, whom Paul described as "the image of the invisible God" (Colossians 1:15).

I hope that many of you reading this book will disagree with me. My desire is for these pages to serve as a catalyst for your continuing adventure, to somehow stir your own hunger for discovery, even if some of my examples or references are difficult to embrace. I have discovered that many of the treasures I write about can be found in different traditions. However, my greatest experience and awareness has come through the pages of the Holy Bible and the fellowship of believers in Christ, and it is in this context that I will seek to unearth these treasures.

At the center of spiritual mining is the gem of faith. The writer of Hebrews tells us that "faith is being sure of what we hope for and certain of what we do not see" (Hebrews 11:1). It is a "sixth" sense, going beyond what we can comprehend with our five physical senses. It is something deeper than emotion or intellect. It is both a decision to trust and a divine intervention in your life. In his adaptation of the New Testament, entitled *The Message*, Eugene Peterson wrote, "Before you trust you have to listen. But unless Christ's Word is preached, there's nothing to listen to." He continues,

> It's the word of faith that welcomes God to go to work and set things right for us. This is the core of our preaching. Say the welcoming word of God—"Jesus is

my Master"—embracing, body and soul, God's work of doing in us what he did in raising Jesus from the dead. That's it. You're not "doing" anything; you're simply calling out to God, trusting him to do it for you. That's salvation. With your whole being you embrace God setting things right, and then you say it, right out loud: "God has set everything right between him and me!" Scripture reassures us, "No one who trusts God like this—heart and soul—will ever regret it." It's exactly the same no matter what a person's religious background may be: the same God for all of us, acting the same incredibly generous way to everyone who calls out for help. Everyone who calls, "Help, God!" gets help.

Faith is taking a risk, investing your future in something and someone greater than yourself. In what many have fondly called the "faith chapter," Hebrews 11:6 teaches us that "without faith it is impossible to please God, because anyone who comes to him must believe that he exists and that he rewards those who earnestly seek him." The New Testament writer James reinforces this by stating, "If any of you lacks wisdom, he should ask God, who gives generously to all without finding fault, and it will be given to him. But when he asks, he must believe and not doubt, because he who doubts is like a wave of the sea, blown and tossed by the wind" (James 1:5–6). This passage is such a powerful statement about the treasure of faith! How can any of us claim lack of wisdom as an excuse when we are encouraged that God gives generously to all without finding fault?

My initial steps of faith were completely ignorant and timid. I hungered to know if God was real and, if He was, what that should mean to me. I explored several religious and secular philosophies, hoping to find purpose and context for my life. I wanted to discover faith in my own way, but I continually found myself trapped in my intellect and emotions. It was satisfying intermittently, but somewhere deeper in my soul I knew it couldn't be real unless it was something bigger than me. If God was real, He couldn't just be a creation of my imagination. I wanted to be arrested by some great spiritual

experience, to be confronted with some physical manifestation
of the reality of God. It wasn't until I became as a little child
that I discovered this treasure. And it was so simple that I
wasn't even aware of the power of faith when it first awakened
me.

My experience wasn't entirely unique. For many people, the
initial steps into faith can be confusing, uncertain, and filled
with questioning as they try to figure out what genuine
spirituality is. For example, one night Jesus was visited by one
of the leaders of the Jewish ruling council, Nicodemus. Let's
listen in on their conversation (adapted from John 3):

Nicodemus: "We know you are a teacher who has come from
God. No one could perform the miracles we have seen you
perform if God wasn't with him."

Jesus: "Let Me give you the truth, Nicodemus: No one can see
the kingdom of God unless he goes through a rebirth."

Nicodemus: "I don't understand." [He understood more than
he was letting on.] "Can a person be reborn when he is old?
You can't be talking about a person jumping back into his
mother's womb?"

Jesus: "I will pretend I didn't hear you say that. Let Me give
you the truth you are seeking again: No one can enter the
kingdom of God unless he is born both by his mother and by
the Spirit, who is above. Sure you have been born in the flesh,
but you also have to be born of the Spirit. This shouldn't
surprise you, Nicodemus. It is much like the wind—you can't
actually see it, but you see its effect. It seems to blow wherever
it wants and you really don't know where it is going to go
next. It is the same way with anyone being born of the Spirit."

Nicodemus: "How can this be? This doesn't seem to fit with
our traditions."

Jesus: "Here you are a religious teacher and you can't
understand this simple beginning of spiritual life? Believe me,

Nicodemus, I know what I'm talking about, and yet you still can't accept what I'm saying. Remember, you started this conversation by saying that you know I am from God because of the miracles you have watched Me perform. I'm just scratching the surface by putting it in a context you can readily understand, and yet you still can't accept it. What if I started telling you things about heaven that can't even be compared with anything here on earth—what would you say then? Let's try just a little: No one has ever gone into heaven up to this point, except for Me and that is because I came from heaven! How does that fit with your religious tradition? Do you remember the story of the Israelites rebelling against Moses and God in the desert and being attacked by venomous snakes? Remember what God told Moses to do in order to save the people? He instructed Moses to make a bronze snake and put it on a pole in front of the people. Whoever looked at the bronze snake survived, and those who refused to look at the snake on the pole died. Think about that story and one day you will figure out who I am. The truth is, Nicodemus, that God loved the world so much that He sent Me so that whoever believes in Me will never die, but will be born of the Spirit and will enjoy life forever. He didn't send Me here to condemn everybody—instead, He sent Me so that everyone who believes in Me could escape condemnation and be saved from misery and destruction. Whoever chooses to believe in Me is already guaranteed life, but if you choose to not believe in Me, you bring condemnation on yourself. So this is the final conclusion of our discussion, Nicodemus, since you are seeking truth: Spiritual light has come into the world, but people prefer darkness instead of light because so many of their past actions have been wrong. Everyone who does bad things hates the light because it exposes them for who they really are. But if you are really seeking truth you will come into the light, and the light itself will show that you have chosen to do the will of God."

True spiritual treasures confront, challenge, and change us. They don't help us justify or rationalize our current condition; instead, they offer a way out of our current condition through the love, dependability, and wisdom of a God bigger than our imagination or religious tradition. Theology is like reading a review of a great show that took place in your hometown last night. You can read about the show and you might even pretend to have been there, but your experience isn't real. Faith is getting a front row seat and backstage pass to spend time with the star of the show! The real substance of your experience can never be captured in the newspaper story (theology). In my own journey, it wasn't until I faced my imperfections and failures that I stumbled into a revelation of the solution: being born of the Spirit. My spiritual breakthrough came when I prayed the following:

> God, I know You are real and I realize that I cannot make any demands on You because I have failed in so many different ways. I know I have failed myself, so I must have failed You even more in ways that I'm not even aware of right now. I guess the only chance I have to know You and be accepted by You is to ask for Your forgiveness and to accept that Jesus died for my sins. Please help me to understand and to hear Your voice in my spirit. I don't know how yet, but I want to give my life to you and I want to learn to hear You and obey You so that I can fulfill Your purpose for my life. Thank You for accepting me even while I'm at my worst, and thank You for taking charge of my life from this point on. In Jesus' name, amen.

That prayer wasn't deep or very enlightened. But because it was the pathway God created for anyone to begin a relationship with Him, it worked. For more than thirty years I have continued that adventure and I can say with total confidence, "No one who trusts God like this—heart and soul—will ever regret it."

Action Steps

1. Write out a list of every mistake or wrong behavior you can remember committing. When you have finished writing out this list of "sins," pray the following prayer:

God, thank You for offering to take away all the guilt associated with these sins I have listed. Though I don't understand it very well yet, I believe that You sent Jesus to show me the way and to carry my burdens so that I can be free to enjoy Your love. I give Jesus all of the guilt for these sins, and I ask for Your guidance and leadership in my life from this day forward. Amen.

Then burn up your list or tear it into small pieces and throw it away, making a conscious decision to accept God's forgiveness and to forgive yourself.

2. Read the eleventh chapter of Hebrews in the New Testament every day for a week and meditate on how faith changed the lives of the people described in this chapter. (If you don't own a Bible, e-mail us at info@lifequestintl.com and we will send you a free copy.)

3. Make a list of how a faith like the kind described in Hebrews 11 has changed your life so far or might change your life in the future.

Points to Ponder

"True faith causes man to acknowledge his own limitations. True faith distinguishes between those things which are within the province of man and those which are within the province of God. Someone has stated the relationship between man's part and God's part in the life of faith as follows: 'You do the simple thing; God will do the complicated thing. You do the small thing; God will do the great thing. You do the possible thing; God will do the impossible thing." — Derek Prince, *The Spirit-Filled Believer's Handbook*

"Being born of the Spirit means much more than we generally take it to mean. It gives us a new vision and keeps us absolutely fresh for everything by the perennial supply of the life of God." — Oswald Chambers, *My Utmost for His Highest*

"Unbelief is abnormal; belief is normal. For the normal human being will joyfully embrace faith and belief, but the cynical doubter cannot believe and will not believe until he can be healed of the negative memories that plague him and block him from his innate ability to see God." — Robert H. Schuller, *The Be-Happy Attitudes*

"I have so much to do that I must spend several hours in
prayer before I am able to do it."
— John Wesley, founder of the Methodist movement

Because so many people have believed in and practiced the
discipline of prayer for so long, some researchers have
undertaken the challenge of attempting to quantify the benefits
of prayer. For instance, Herbert Benson, an associate professor
at Harvard Medical School, found that people can decrease
their blood pressure, heart rate, and breathing rates through
prayer. Randolph Byrd, a cardiologist at the University of
California at San Francisco, divided three hundred and ninety-
three heart patients randomly into two groups. One group
received standard medical care. The other also received the
daily prayers of volunteers who described themselves as born-
again Christians. The patients, the hospital staff, and Byrd did
not know who was prayed for and who wasn't. The study
found that patients singled out for prayer required fewer
antibiotics, suffered less congestive heart failure, and were less
likely to develop pneumonia. In 1990 researchers from
Northwestern University Medical School found that among
elderly women who had hip surgery, those with a strong
religious faith got back on their feet faster than did
nonbelievers.

Some scientists have postulated that the benefits of prayer come
from within the person praying. They suggest the mere practice
of asking for help, or meditating about our blessings, the
wonders of creation, and so on have a positive effect on the
mental well-being of the participant, regardless of what else
may be happening. Of course, most spiritual leaders consider
this far too superficial of an explanation of what is taking place.
They believe that prayer is an expression of an interpersonal
relationship between the person praying and his Creator. I have
concluded they are both correct. In my life, prayer has been

both a tremendous source of personal growth and a wonderful time of interaction with God. I agree with the statement of Lord Tennyson: "More things are wrought by prayer than this world dreams of."

While studying this subject, I ventured onto the Internet to see what it could teach me about prayer. To my surprise, I found 1,476,970 Web sites on prayer! And that was only using one search engine! There are a number of quotes about prayer that have been sources of encouragement to me through the years. Here are just a few:

Charles Trumbull said, "Prayer is releasing the energies of God. For prayer is asking God to do what we cannot do."

Moody Monthly had this to say about prayer: "It is not the arithmetic of our prayers, how many they are; nor the rhetoric of our prayers, how eloquent they be; nor the geometry of our prayers, how long they may be; nor the music of our prayers, how sweet our voice may be; nor the logic of our prayers, how argumentative they may be; nor the method of our prayers, how orderly they may be; or even the theology of our prayers, how good the doctrine—which God cares for. Fervency of spirit is that which availeth much."

I also ran across this beautiful verse about prayer (author unknown):

> Prayer is so simple;
> It is like quietly opening a door
> And slipping into the very presence of God,
> There in the stillness
> To listen to His voice;
> Perhaps to petition,
> Or only to listen;
> It matters not.
> Just to be there
> In His presence
> Is prayer.

Probably my favorite thoughts about the power of prayer come from children. For example, a young boy was overheard praying, "Lord, if You can't make me a better boy, don't worry about it. I'm having a real good time as it is." And a simple prayer that reveals a great friendship between a little girl and God was overheard: "And, dear God, I hope You'll also take care of Yourself. If anything should happen to You, we'd be in an awful fix."

Prayer was a vital part of Jesus' life on earth. The Scriptures reveal that many times He rose early before sunrise and went out alone to pray. How is it that Someone who was supposed to be the incarnation of God still needed to pray? Was it because through His becoming the Son of Man He intentionally put Himself in our shoes, limiting His resources to the same available to us—through prayer? His followers asked him to teach them how to pray. Most people raised in a Christian culture are familiar with the prayer He taught (Matthew 6:9–13, KJV):

> Our Father which art in heaven,
> Hallowed be thy name.
> Thy kingdom come.
> Thy will be done in earth, as it is in heaven.
> Give us this day our daily bread.
> And forgive us our debts, as we forgive our debtors.
> And lead us not into temptation, but deliver us from evil:
> For thine is the kingdom, and the power, and the glory, for ever.
> Amen.

This prayer provides a simple but comprehensive model for how to pray. However, before examining the Lord's Prayer, let's look at Eugene Peterson's adaptation of this same prayer from *The Message*:

> Our Father in heaven,
> Reveal who you are.
> Set the world right:

Do what's best—as above, so below.
Keep us alive with three square meals.
Keep us forgiven with you and forgiving others.
Keep us safe from ourselves and the Devil.
You're in charge!
You can do anything you want!
You're ablaze in beauty!
Yes. Yes. Yes.

Through this prayer, Jesus taught His disciples—and us—a pattern to follow when we pray.

"Our Father which art in heaven, hallowed be thy name." Jesus' model begins with recognizing and acknowledging God for who He is. The psalmist wrote it this way in Psalm 100:4: "Enter his gates with thanksgiving and his courts with praise." We begin to "condition" ourselves for communion with God first by giving thanks for all that He has done and giving Him praise for who He is. It isn't that He is starved for attention or in need of getting His ego stroked. Starting with this recognition helps us to approach our communion with God without being presumptuous or self-centered. Thanksgiving and praise help us to unpack the emotional grime that we pick up throughout life and provides a spiritual shower to cleanse our thoughts and emotions before having fellowship with Him.

"Thy kingdom come. Thy will be done in earth, as it is in heaven." This part of Jesus' model gives us the basis for great faith in addressing the obstacles in our lives. Jesus was teaching His disciples that praying according to God's will was the key to seeing amazing results. It isn't about taking a to-do list to God and treating Him like a vending machine. Instead, Jesus told His disciples, "If you remain in me and my words remain in you, ask whatever you wish, and it will be given you" (John 15:7) and, "Have faith in God . . . . I tell you the truth, if anyone says to this mountain, 'Go, throw yourself into the sea,' and does not doubt in his heart but believes that what he says will happen, it will be done for him. Therefore I tell you, whatever you ask for in prayer, believe that you have received it, and it will be yours" (Mark 11:22–24). I have used this part of Jesus'

prayer model to pray, "Your kingdom come in me as it is in heaven. Your kingdom come in my family as it is in heaven. Your kingdom come in our country as it is in heaven. Your kingdom come in my business as it is in heaven," and so on. It is a blanket invitation for God to invade your life and to bring His goodness and purpose to fruition in you.

"*Give us this day our daily bread.*" This part of the prayer model teaches us to present all of our needs to God and to trust for His daily provision. Jesus instructed His followers, "Do not worry about your life, what you will eat or drink; or about your body, what you will wear. Is not life more important than food, and the body more important than clothes? . . . But seek first his kingdom and his righteousness, and all these things will be given to you as well" (Matthew 6:25, 33). Paul restates this principle in Philippians 4:6–7: "Do not be anxious for anything, but in everything, by prayer and petition, with thanksgiving, present your requests to God. And the peace of God, which transcends all understanding, will guard your hearts and your minds in Christ Jesus."

"*And forgive us our debts, as we forgive our debtors.*" We will look at the treasure of forgiveness in a later chapter, but it is essential to realize that in prayer there is a connection between what God does and what we do. It is very sobering to realize that if we choose to not forgive, we cut ourselves off from the forgiveness of God. Jesus taught us that the cost of an unforgiving spirit is too high, even under the worst possible mistreatment from others. While suffering an unjust punishment of crucifixion on the cross, He still chose to pray, "Father, forgive them, for they do not know what they are doing" (Luke 23:24).

"*And lead us not into temptation, but deliver us from evil.*" Jesus perceived a continual battle within each of us between good and evil. He recognized the temptations of appetite, presumption, and illegitimate power because these were the exact temptations He faced during and after His forty days of fasting in the desert. The original Scripture texts are written, "deliver us from the evil *one*" (emphasis mine), referring to a spiritual antagonist to the purposes of God. In teaching us to pray this way, Jesus extended the battle between good and evil beyond our internal struggles to include a spiritual conflict that involves beings beyond the human arena. To the modern scientific mind, this sounds like old-fashioned superstition and mythology. However, as a pastor that has sought to help hundreds of people with problems that mere counseling and therapy could not solve, I discovered that doing battle against external evil forces is often the key to victory. The writer of Hebrews adds to our understanding of God's desire to assist us by writing, "Therefore, since we have a great high priest who has gone through the heavens, Jesus the Son of God, let us hold firmly to the faith we profess. For we do not have a high priest who is unable to sympathize with our weaknesses, but we have one who has been tempted in every way, just as we are—yet was without sin. Let us then approach the throne of grace with confidence, so that we may receive mercy and find grace to help us in our time of need" (Hebrews 4:14–16).

"For thine is the kingdom, and the power, and the glory, for ever. Amen." After lifting our needs, concerns, and temptations to God in prayer, Jesus reminds us to leave these burdens in God's hands, recognizing that there is no exhausting His resources or desire to answer our prayers.

If all that the bible teaches about prayer is true, why do we so often fail to realize the fulfillment of our prayers? Anyone who has given much effort to prayer can point to some prayers that don't seem to get answered. Some qualifiers are given throughout the Bible to help us understand the imperfect nature of this exploration of prayer. First, Jesus taught that prayer must be persistent. To capture the original language (Greek) of the Book of Luke, Jesus told His disciples to "ask and keep on asking, and it shall be given you; seek and keep on seeking, and you shall find; knock and keep on knocking, and the door shall be opened" (11:9, *The Amplified Bible*). I believe the most common reason for unanswered prayer is lack of persistence. A great example of this is found in Luke 18:1 (*The Message*):

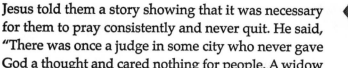
Jesus told them a story showing that it was necessary for them to pray consistently and never quit. He said, "There was once a judge in some city who never gave God a thought and cared nothing for people. A widow in that city kept after him: 'My rights are being violated. Protect me!' He never gave her the time of day. But after this went on and on he said to himself, 'I care nothing what God thinks, even less what people think. But because this widow won't quit badgering me, I'd better do something and see that she gets justice—otherwise I'm going to end up beaten black-and-blue by her pounding.'" Then the Master said, "Do you hear what that judge, corrupt as he is, is saying? So what makes you think God won't step in and work justice for his chosen people, who continue to cry out for help? Won't he stick up for them? I assure you, he will. He will not drag his feet. But how much of that kind of persistent faith will the Son of Man find on the earth when he returns?"

Another reason for unanswered prayer revealed in Scripture is praying with the wrong motives. James wrote in his New Testament letter, "You do not have because you do not ask God. When you ask, you do not receive, because you ask with wrong motives, that you may spend what you get on your pleasures" (James 4:2–3).

And finally, sometimes our prayers aren't answered because they would abort the purpose of God in our lives. In Gethsemane, as Jesus prepared for His suffering, He prayed, "My Father, if it is possible, may this cup be taken from me. Yet not as I will, but as you will" (Matthew 26:39). It may seem cruel for God to not answer Jesus' prayer or, likewise, to not answer our earnest prayers to protect a loved one from suffering, but we should always keep in mind that we are spiritual explorers during this life, with a much more meaningful life and purpose in the one to come. As painful as this life can be, God has a perspective rooted in eternity that recognizes the purpose and brevity of suffering during our time on earth. If we can reach out in faith, there are treasures to be found in suffering that are too precious and mysterious to understand apart from divine illumination.

At its core, prayer is simply cultivating and enjoying a relationship with God. We learn from the example and instructions of Jesus and we grow in this relationship as our faith grows one day at a time. One of the most powerful prayer exercises I have discovered is the practice of writing out my prayers as a two-way conversation with God. Here is an example:

> Ron: "Good morning, Lord."

> Lord: "Good morning, Ron."

> Ron: "I love You, Lord. Thank You for adopting me into Your family. Thank You for cleansing me from all of the mistakes I have made. Thank You for giving me this opportunity to spend time with You today."

> Lord: "You're welcome, Ron. I love you and I want to show you more of Myself today. Come close to Me in faith. Open up your heart to me and I will speak words of encouragement to you."

I use my computer to capture these times of fellowship together, and they have increased my faith tremendously. Of course, I don't consider these prayer logs to be infallible, nor do I consider myself to be a perfect listener—they are simply an experiment to help me grow in my spiritual receptivity. Over time, they have helped to open up my spiritual ears to enjoy a more intimate relationship with God.

How about you? Would you like to have a daily appointment with the Creator of the universe? If it were possible, would you want to develop an intimate, unique relationship with God Almighty? Would you consider that a treasure worth pursuing? If so, He is waiting for you to come on in—through prayer.

Action Steps

1. Using the model of the Lord's Prayer, write out a prayer letter to God. For instance, for "Our Father which art in heaven, hallowed be thy name," make a list of things you are thankful to God for and attributes for which He is worthy of praise. For "Thy kingdom come. Thy will be done in earth, as it is in heaven," make a list of areas in your life where you want His kingdom to be manifested, and so on.

2. Find a place of solitude and spend at least thirty minutes each day quieting your mind from all the worries and concerns of daily living. Sit in God's presence and commune with Him, learning how to speak to Him as a friend and listening for messages to be dropped into your heart. Spend ten minutes of this time reading through the Book of Mark in the New Testament.

3. Experiment with writing out your prayers as a two-way conversation between you and God. Write whatever comes to your mind, with the goal of developing a relationship and slowly learning how to hear with a heart of faith.

Points to Ponder

"Prayer is the most important thing in my life. If I should neglect prayer for a single day, I should lose a great deal of the fire of faith." — Martin Luther

"Prayer is not overcrowding God's reluctance, but taking hold of God's willingness." — Anonymous

"Don't pray for tasks equal to your powers, but powers equal to your tasks." — Anonymous

Chapter 26
Confession

"Last night my little boy confessed to me some childish
wrong;
And kneeling at my knee he prayed with tears—
'Dear God, make me a man like Daddy—wise and strong. I
know You can.'
Then while he slept I knelt beside his bed, confessed my
sins, and prayed with low-bowed head,
'O God, make me a child like my child here—
pure, guileless, trusting Thee with faith sincere."
— Author unknown

In my quest for spiritual treasures, I often catch myself repeating the phrase "Oh, what a tangled web we weave," as I observe the many ups and downs of seeking a life of maturity and fulfillment. For most of us, moving into adulthood and parenthood and then coming to grips with our mortality on earth is an increasingly complicated process. When we are young, we think we understand ourselves and the world around us. We develop a philosophy of living and we "go for the gusto" in everything we do. Some refer to this as the age of innocence. As life unfolds, we begin to discover that life isn't as simple as we imagined, that some of our philosophies don't fit into reality too well, and that there are a whole lot of people who disagree with our road map for living. Most challenging of all, we begin to discover cracks in our character, whether through overt sins or more subtle failures to live up to our own standards of conduct. We find we need something to lift us out of the quagmire created by our experiences.

One of the spiritual treasures available to lift us from this bog of confusion, disappointment, and failure is confession. What do you think of when you hear the word *confession*? Do you think of going to a priest and admitting to having broken some rule of the church? Do you think of the people who pour out of their seats at a Billy Graham crusade to make a decision for

Christ? Do you think of a suspect breaking down under intense interrogation to admit that he is guilty of the crime?

None of these represent the spiritual treasure of which I'm speaking. Confession is a much more powerful treasure than these examples. We can begin to discover the power of confession by looking at its original meaning. Both the English word and its Greek counterpart found in the original language of the New Testament mean literally, "saying the same as." In other words, in a spiritual context, confession means "to agree with God." Another important implication in this definition is to speak out loud, as opposed to silent prayer or meditation (which have their own value). To recognize the potential power in this confession, let's look at what the apostle Paul says in his letter to the church of Rome:

> Brothers, my heart's desire and prayer to God for the Israelites is that they may be saved. For I can testify about them that they are zealous for God, but their zeal is not based on knowledge. Since they did not know the righteousness that comes from God and sought to establish their own, they did not submit to God's righteousness. Christ is the end of the law so that there may be righteousness for everyone who believes. . . . But what does it say? "The word is near you; it is in your mouth and in your heart," that is, the word of faith we are proclaiming: That if you confess with your mouth, "Jesus is Lord," and believe in your heart that God raised him from the dead, you will be saved. For it is with your heart that you believe and are justified, and it is with your mouth that you confess and are saved. (Romans 10:1–4, 8–10)

In this passage, we can clearly see that confession is by no means limited to admission of guilt, but is a process of agreeing with God first in our heart and then with our tongue. There is a relationship between what we believe in our heart and what comes out of our mouth that uncovers spiritual treasure. Jesus taught it this way:

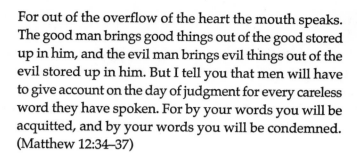

For out of the overflow of the heart the mouth speaks. The good man brings good things out of the good stored up in him, and the evil man brings evil things out of the evil stored up in him. But I tell you that men will have to give account on the day of judgment for every careless word they have spoken. For by your words you will be acquitted, and by your words you will be condemned. (Matthew 12:34–37)

Wow! Are our words really that powerful, that on the basis of our words judgment will be rendered? If we really believe this, how might it change the way we use our words? The wise king Solomon wrote hundreds of years before Jesus, "The tongue has the power of life and death, and those who love it will eat its fruit" and, "Reckless words pierce like a sword, but the tongue of the wise brings healing" (Proverbs 18:21, 12:18). In the Bible's account of creation, we learn that God *spoke* the worlds into existence. It is clear from the Scriptures that great power has been given to us through our confession and, depending on how we use this power, we can unearth great treasures.

There are two primary areas of agreement with God that we would do well to include in our confessions. The first relates to the nature of sin and our experience with it. The second relates to the nature of righteousness and God's love in our lives. Both of these may seem awkward and difficult for us at first. However, they can become a source of great strength and transformation when made a regular part of our daily lives. And as we discover the power that confession has in our own lives, we can use this power to bless the lives of those around us.

During the early days of my spiritual journey, it was difficult to agree with God regarding the nature of sin. I wanted to believe that I was fundamentally good (after all, I was created in His image) and I just made mistakes now and then. I was willing to admit that I sinned from time to time, but I resisted the idea that at my core I was a sinner. Likewise, I wanted to believe that mankind was basically good and that most misconduct was a matter of poor environmental conditioning. When I read Scriptures like, "There is no one righteous, not even one" (Romans 3:10), or, "All men are liars" (Psalm 116:11), I had a difficult time accepting this biblical analysis of mankind. My man-centered philosophy denied the scriptural revelation that we are all born with a fatal flaw described by theologians as original sin. This doctrine explains that because of genetic inheritance, we are all born with a proclivity to rebel against God and to sin. This seemed unfair to me, so I wrestled with it and tried to deny its reality. It took years of disappointment before I was willing to agree that the Scriptures contain an accurate description of God's diagnosis.

It sounds silly to say that I didn't agree with God, doesn't it? However, it wasn't until I began to accept this judgment that I found the freedom and power I was seeking. This is one of the fundamental ways that Christianity differs from the other religions I have studied. Other religions continue to urge the development of self-righteousness through discipline and self-actualization. They urge us to pursue an inner hunger for divinity and to set aside lower appetites that may hinder our evolution into "becoming gods." Essentially, they remain self-centered and self-fueled with the assistance of a Buddha or some other leader to serve as a spiritual guide.

In contrast, authentic Christianity (there are plenty of religious leaders peddling a self-centered version of Christianity) urges us to give up trying to achieve self-righteousness and to look for another kind of righteousness that originates in a transaction completed by God at the cross. Authentic Christianity gives us to the freedom to lay down our burden to perform and evolve through self-effort and, instead, invites us to receive a free gift of acceptance, righteousness, and wholeness through the acknowledgement of our sinful nature and through faith in Christ. Its goal is still transformation, but the path to change is no longer based on self-effort. Instead, change comes about simply as a result of agreeing with God.

Most of us will try everything else before surrendering to the power of confession. We will attempt to convince ourselves

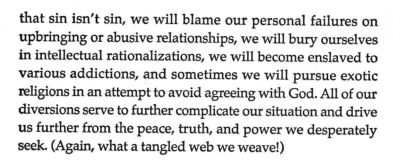

that sin isn't sin, we will blame our personal failures on upbringing or abusive relationships, we will bury ourselves in intellectual rationalizations, we will become enslaved to various addictions, and sometimes we will pursue exotic religions in an attempt to avoid agreeing with God. All of our diversions serve to further complicate our situation and drive us further from the peace, truth, and power we desperately seek. (Again, what a tangled web we weave!)

Even when we have made a clear commitment to God through Christ and we call ourselves followers of Jesus, we often continue to seek self-made righteousness and we engage in subtle delusions that make life miserable both for us and those we love. My heart aches for many of my friends because I suspect that the primary obstacle to their discovery of grace is injury and disillusionment experienced at the hands of other Christians, who became perpetrators because of their own failure to properly engage the power of confession.

So, how can confession of sin release treasure into our lives? First, confession is a source of great treasure because recognition of the truth brings us freedom. When we agree with God's definition of sin, we align ourselves with reality. When we confess our sins we free ourselves from the burden of guilt, alienation, and estrangement from a pure and holy God. We return to the naked truth that we are all sinners and rebellious by nature, afflicted by an inherited flaw that cannot be overcome by our own efforts, regardless of how noble they may be. In acknowledging our failure through confession, we position ourselves to receive God's solution to a problem that can be solved only by divine intervention. We are refreshed by the mercies of God, which Scripture tells us are renewed every morning throughout our lives. These mercies are God's decisions not to give us what we deserve (the judgment that sin elicits), but to give us what we don't deserve (just as if we had never sinned). Through faith in God's provision for us, we become partakers of grace, which is the enabling presence of God, empowering us to become what we were created to be according to His kind desires toward us. Therefore, we read in Hebrews 4:16, "Let us approach the throne of grace with confidence, so that we may receive mercy and find grace to help us in our time of need."

If confession regarding sin brings freedom and peace to our lives, confession of God's intentions, love, and new life for us is truly transformational. Consider the following perspectives of God regarding our lives in Christ:

> Therefore, if anyone is in Christ, he is a new creation; the old has gone, the new has come! All this is from God, who reconciled us to himself through Christ and gave us the ministry of reconciliation: that God was reconciling the world to himself in Christ, not counting men's sins against them. And he has committed to us the message of reconciliation. We are therefore Christ's ambassadors, as though God were making his appeal through us. We implore you on Christ's behalf: Be reconciled to God. God made him who had no sin to be sin for us, so that in him we might become the righteousness of God. (2 Corinthians 5:17–21)

> And we know that in all things God works for the good of those who love him, who are called according to his purpose. For those God foreknew he also predestined to be conformed to the likeness of his Son, that he might be the firstborn among many brothers. And those he predestined, he also called; those he called, he also justified; those he justified, he also glorified. What, then, shall we say in response to this? If God is for us, who can be against us? He who did not spare his own Son, but gave him up for us all—how will he not also, along with him, graciously give us all things? (Romans 8:28–32)

> And God raised us up with Christ and seated us with him in heavenly realms in Christ Jesus, in order that in the coming ages he might show the incomparable riches of his grace, expressed in his kindness to us in Christ Jesus. For it is by grace you have been saved, through faith—and this not from yourselves, it is the gift of

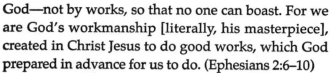

God—not by works, so that no one can boast. For we are God's workmanship [literally, his masterpiece], created in Christ Jesus to do good works, which God prepared in advance for us to do. (Ephesians 2:6–10)

And God is able to make all grace abound to you, so that in all things at all times, having all that you need, you will abound in every good work. (2 Corinthians 9:8)

These are just a few of God's perspectives toward us as a result of our union with His Son. There are hundreds of similar promises throughout the Scriptures that provide untold treasures when we learn to agree with God through confession. Imagine what a transformation would occur if you truly and literally believed and regularly confessed these "God perspectives" about yourself! Too often, however, we rob ourselves of this transformational power because we choose to believe and speak otherwise. Imagine the transformational impact on your relationships if you could start viewing those around you as recipients of this destiny from God.

As we begin to view ourselves from God's perspective and make this part of our regular confession, we effectively invite the presence of God deeper and deeper into our lives. As we agree with Him through confession, we begin to take on His likeness and, over time, achieve the very thing we had hoped to achieve before through self-effort: becoming like God. So the end of the matter is that we really do become partakers of the divine nature, not through the worn-out attempts of self-effort, but as a result of the empowering presence of God. By agreeing with God through confession, we discover an immeasurable field of hidden treasures that can never be depleted or exhausted of its wealth.

So what do you think—is it worth surrendering your independence, intellectual rationalizations, and emotional I.O.U.'s to discover the treasures of God?

Actions Steps

1. Make a list of any sins you have committed and have never confessed to God. Take some time to recount your entire life to make sure there is no sin that hasn't been traded in for God's forgiveness and cleansing.

2. Call a friend or religious leader whom you can trust to hear your confession with compassion and confidentiality. Let them know that you want to get together to share your confession and receive the prayer of forgiveness and then set an appointment to complete your confession. At the end of this appointment, have your counselor tear up your list of sins and completely destroy it as a symbol of forgiveness and cleansing. (Private confession between you and God is also legitimate, but greater power and release often comes through confessing to another trustworthy and compassionate person. See James 5:16 and 1 John 1:8–9.)

3. Copy a list of promises from God found in the Bible that you will read out loud every day for thirty days. Observe how confessing these promises (agreeing with God) begins to transform your life. If you are new to the Bible, highlight and use the verses included in this chapter about God's love and plan for you.

Points to Ponder

"Admitting personal guilt may not be pleasant, but it is a first step towards forgiveness. If a person waded through a mud hole but refused to believe he needed a bath, he might never get clean. If an unkempt person assumed he was well groomed and refused to look at himself in a mirror, he might never shape up. Soap and water and a mirror do nothing for the person who thinks he is clean and dazzling. Similarly, as long as a person refuses to acknowledge his or her sin and guilt, God's love and forgiveness are untapped." — Jim Dyet and Jim Russell, *Overcoming Subtle Sins*

"Christ is called 'the High Priest' of our confession (Hebrews

3:1, NKJV). This means that Christ in heaven serves as our Advocate and Representative in respect to every truth of God's Word to which we on earth confess with our mouth. But whenever we fail to confess our faith on earth, we give Christ no opportunity to act on our behalf in heaven. By closing our lips on earth, we also close the lips of our Advocate in heaven."
— Derek Prince, *The Spirit-Filled Believer's Handbook*

"Do not let any unwholesome talk come out of your mouths, but only what is helpful for building others up according to their needs, that it may benefit those who listen." —Ephesians 4:29

Chapter 27

Repentance

More than thirty years ago, I read a booklet written by Rev. David Duplessis entitled, "God Has No Grandchildren." In this essay, Duplessis explained that the Christian church is always one generation away from disappearing off the face of the earth. He pointed out that authentic Christianity is not based on ritual or institutional tradition, but on individual conversion that must occur one person at a time, generation after generation. Nobody becomes part of the family of God based on someone else's decision or because of their natural family. Therefore, God has millions, probably, billions of children, but no grandchildren.

This concept intrigued me. Though I was brought up in the Christian tradition and I believed in God, I mark my adoption as a child of God by my own conversion experience, which culminated on August 4, 1971. After searching for a connection to God over many years, I prayed something similar to what is commonly referred to as "the sinner's prayer" at approximately 2:00 in the morning. It was not an emotional experience for me, but it was a turning point that changed my life forever. Two vital actions took place early that morning that resulted in my being "born by the Spirit" so that I could see and enter the kingdom of God. These two actions, identified as foundational to reconciliation in the Book of Hebrews, were repentance from dead works (fruitless rituals) and faith toward God.

Derek Prince explains it this way in *The Spirit-Filled Believer's Handbook*:

> The perfect example of true repentance is found in the parable of the prodigal son (see Luke 15:11–32). There we read how the prodigal turned his back on father and home and went off into a distant land, there to waste all that he had in sin and dissipation. Eventually he came

to himself, hungry, lonely and in rags, sitting among the swine, longing for something to fill his stomach. At this point he made a decision. He said, "I will arise and go to my father." He immediately carried out his decision: "And he arose and came to his father." This is true repentance: first, the inward decision; and then the outward act of that decision—the act of turning back to father and home. In his own unregenerate, sinful condition, every man that was ever born has turned his back on God, his Father, and on heaven, his home. Each step he takes is a step away from God and from heaven. As he walks this way, the light is behind him, and the shadows are before him. The farther he goes, the longer and darker the shadows become. Each step he takes is one step nearer the end—one step nearer the grave, nearer hell, nearer the endless darkness of a lost eternity. For every man who takes this course, there is one essential act he must make. He must stop, change his mind, change his direction, face the opposite way, turn his back to the shadows and face toward the light. This first, essential act is called repentance in the scriptures.

As John the Baptist sought to prepare Israel for the coming of the Messiah, his simple message was, "Repent, for the kingdom of heaven is near." When Jesus began his ministry, his first and recurring theme was, "The time has come. . . . The kingdom of God is near. Repent and believe the good news" (Mark 1:15). As Peter sought to share this good news about the kingdom of heaven after the crucifixion and resurrection of Jesus, he told those who would listen, "Now, brothers, I know that you acted in ignorance, as did your leaders. But this is how God fulfilled what he had foretold through all the prophets, saying that his Christ would suffer. Repent, then, and turn to God, that times of refreshing may come from the Lord" (Acts 3:17–19).

What is this repentance and how does it qualify as a diamond of the spirit? In the Hebrew language of the Old Testament, the word for *repentance* means "to turn" or "to turn back." In the Greek language of the New Testament, repentance means "to change one's mind." Interestingly, neither definition

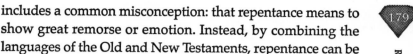

includes a common misconception: that repentance means to show great remorse or emotion. Instead, by combining the languages of the Old and New Testaments, repentance can be described as an inner change of mind that results in an outward change of direction. On August 4, 1971, I made an inner decision to turn away from "salvation by self-help" and to turn toward the simplicity of asking God for forgiveness on the basis that Jesus Christ died for my sins and offers me rebirth into the family of God. This simple act of repentance changed my life. But it was not a once-for-all-time event. It was the beginning of a new way of living. It was recognition of the primary challenge in my life to continually turn toward God and to set aside my ways to pursue his ways. The prophet Isaiah wrote, "Seek the LORD while he may be found; call on him while he is near. Let the wicked forsake his way and the evil man his thoughts. Let him turn to the Lord, and he will have mercy on him, and to our God, for he will freely pardon. 'For my thoughts are not your thoughts, neither are your ways my ways,' declares the LORD. 'As the heavens are higher than the earth, so are my ways higher than your ways and my thoughts than your thoughts'" (Isaiah 55:6–9).

Over the past thirty years, I have found this principle of repentance, or changing my mind followed by a tangible change in direction, to serve my exploration of spiritual treasures over and over again. It is the key to remaining teachable, flexible, and changeable as I seek to continually experience the presence of God—and, therefore, become more like Him.

A great example of the concept of repentance can be seen in the admonition to "forgive those who trespass against us." The Bible, as well as almost every other sacred writing of the world's religions, contains strong exhortations to forgive those who commit an injustice against us. And for good reason: resentment, combined with an unforgiving spirit, is probably the single greatest cause of estrangement and emotional suffering today, often expanding its tentacles beyond our emotional well-being, poisoning our spiritual and physical health as well.

It is easy to talk of forgiveness in theoretical terms or to see the damage resentment wreaks in the lives of those around us. However, it can be quite a different matter when the resentment resides within us. Most of the time, we hold onto resentment because we believe the offending party has done us a serious wrong and we have a justifiable right to hold an emotional I.O.U. against them. We store this resentment because it justifies our rejection of their friendship and relieves us of any obligation for their future well-being. Rarely will anyone sufficiently pay back the emotional debt they have incurred with us, so we "hold the note" as a defense against future demands.

The Scriptures are so clear about the devastating effect an unforgiving attitude has in our lives, however, that there is no logical rationalization to hold onto resentment. At the same time, forgiveness is one of the hardest spiritual disciplines to consistently practice. That's why we need repentance. By recognizing the destructive nature of resentment, we can make an inner decision to change our mind about the offending person. Then, we can complete repentance by turning away from resentment and taking some action that expresses our turning toward God and extending forgiveness. Sometimes, this act of repentance will need to be repeated over and over again to achieve complete freedom. From Eugene Peterson's *The Message* we read:

> Peter got up the nerve to ask, "Master, how many times do I forgive a brother or sister who hurts me? Seven?" Jesus replied, "Seven! Hardly. Try seventy times seven. The kingdom of God is like a king who decided to square accounts with his servants. As he got under way, one servant was brought before him who had run up a debt of a hundred thousand dollars. He couldn't pay up, so the king ordered the man, along with his wife, children, and goods, to be auctioned off at the slave market. The poor wretch threw himself at the king's feet and begged, 'Give me a chance and I'll pay it back.' Touched by his plea, the king let him off, erasing the debt. The servant

was no sooner out of the room when he came upon one of his fellow servants who owed him ten dollars. He seized him by the throat and demanded, 'Pay up. Now!' The poor wretch threw himself down and begged, 'Give me a chance and I'll pay it back.' But he wouldn't do it. He had him arrested and put in jail until the debt was paid. When the other servants saw this going on, they were outraged and brought a detailed report to the king. The king summoned the man and said, 'You evil servant! I forgave your entire debt when you begged me for mercy. Shouldn't you be compelled to be merciful to your fellow servant who asked for mercy?' The king was furious and put the screws to the man until he paid back his entire debt. And that's exactly what my Father in heaven is going to do to each one of you who doesn't forgive unconditionally anyone who asks for mercy." (Matthew 18:21–35)

Of course, if we are looking for a way out of forgiveness, we might point out that in this story Jesus made forgiveness mandatory only when the offender asks us for it. Many other Scriptures eliminate this escape hatch and make it abundantly clear that we forgive others to free ourselves from the destructive poison of resentment. And the key to forgiveness is repentance.

A tremendous example of the power in repentance for forgiveness is the story of Corrie Ten Boom, author of *The Hiding Place*. Corrie was a young Lutheran girl from Denmark whose family hid Jewish people in their attic during World War II. When they were discovered, they were shipped off to death camps and Corrie watched her sister suffer at the hands of a particularly cruel guard. Years later a man came up to Corrie in a church service and introduced himself; he was the guard responsible for her dear sister's death. With every fiber in her body wanting revenge, Corrie found the power of repentance, and against all human emotion extended her love and forgiveness to this man, who had since become part of the family of God. Could you do the same?

Another example of the power of repentance can be discovered as we navigate the battles and challenges of daily life. We live in an imperfect world and we are still going through the process of transformation. Some days we experience tremendous advances, and other days it seems everything we have been seeking to accomplish in our spiritual journey falls apart. There are seasons of growth and seasons of stagnation. There are times of great victory over temptation and, sooner or later, there will be times when we falter and succumb. Some of us have seasons of subtly drifting away from the presence of God, and others consciously and shamelessly rebel against the truth. Whether these failures are great or small, repentance always gives us a road back. We begin by confessing our sin, then we make an inner decision to change, followed by an outward turning away from our waywardness to move back toward God's mercy and grace. There is a song I regularly sing as a reminder of how easy it is to turn back and return to God's favor:

> The steadfast love of the Lord never ceases,
> His mercies never come to an end.
> They are new every morning, new every morning,
> Great is thy faithfulness, O Lord, great is thy faithfulness.
> (adapted from Lamentations 3:22–23, KJV)

I am also regularly reminded of 1 John 1:7: "If we walk in the light, as he is in the light, we have fellowship with one another, and the blood of Jesus, his Son, purifies us from all sin." Two verses later we read, "If we confess our sins, he is faithful and just and will forgive us our sins and purify us from all unrighteousness." The original language of these verses clearly communicates that the blood of Jesus (His sacrifice on our behalf) is continually cleansing us from all sin, rather than only being available at the point of our original confession of faith. To receive this cleansing, we need only to turn back to the light through confession, repentance, and fellowship with one another.

Action Steps

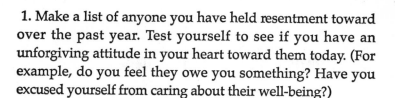

1. Make a list of anyone you have held resentment toward over the past year. Test yourself to see if you have an unforgiving attitude in your heart toward them today. (For example, do you feel they owe you something? Have you excused yourself from caring about their well-being?)

2. Look at the people on your list and begin to pray for blessings in their lives every day until you begin to sense the warmth of God's love toward them in your heart. This helps you to understand the power and transformation available through repentance.

3. Are there other struggles in your life where you need to enlist the spiritual power of repentance? What would repentance look like in these situations? What change of mind will it require? What new actions should you take to turn away from darkness and turn back toward God. Whom can you ask to hold you accountable to take these actions? Create a plan to complete this repentance as soon as possible and without allowing any exceptions to occur until your turning back to God is complete.

Points to Ponder

"So that morning I said, 'God, what am I going to do? I believe I'm right; she believes she's right. I think she's wrong, and I know You know she's wrong, but You won't help me.' Then He asked me the question, 'Do you want to be right, or do you want to be reconciled?' As much as I hated the question, I knew the answer." — Joseph L. Garlington, *Right or Reconciled?*

"When our weakness (or sin) is exposed, we can either admit it, repent, and be cleansed and forgiven—as David was—or we can hide, cling to our reputation among our peers, and fail in the problem." — Bob Mumford, *The Purpose of Temptation*

"If we claim to be without sin, we deceive ourselves and the truth is not in us. If we confess our sins, he is faithful and just and will forgive us our sins and purify us from all un-righteousness." — 1 John 1:8–9

Chapter 28
Worship

"Worship is a deliberate and disciplined adventure in
reality."
— Willard Sperry

Just as we were made to eat, drink, breathe, move, sleep, and
love, we were made to worship. Something deep in all of us
longs to worship, to adore, and to revere. It will—it must—
find expression in our lives. Some of us express this need
through our admiration of creation, whether it is mountains,
rain forests, the oceans, or the stars. Some worship the arts as
an expression of the world around us. Some of us express
worship by "deifying" a person—there are plenty of love songs
to corroborate this. Some of us worship past spiritual or
national leaders, often by celebrating an altered image of who
and what they were. Some worship ancestors in hope of
gaining better treatment in this life as well as the life to come.
Some worship a broad assortment of "gods," depending on
the need or experience of the moment. Some of us are bold
enough to worship ourselves, thinking that we are ascending
into divinity through our personal investments in education,
enlightenment, and self-development. We all express worship
in one way or another—it is a part of us.

It is interesting that, of the Ten Commandments God gave to
Moses for the Israelites after they left Egypt, the first four dealt
with their relationship to God and the remaining six addressed
how they were to relate to one another. The four commandments
addressing their relationship to God, paraphrased, are:

1. I am your God, I rescued you—don't worship any
others.
2. Don't make idols of any kind, no matter how beautiful
they may be. I'm a jealous God and I want all of your
love. People who oppose Me will bring suffering not
only on themselvesbut also on three or four generations

afterwards. On the otherhand, I will lavish my love on those who love and obey Me for one thousand generations!

3. Don't misuse My name—doing so is going to cause you problems.

4. Take every seventh day to rest and spend time with Me. I made the universe in six days and then I rested, so you should do the same. The seventh day is a time to enjoy My blessings in your life.

The Old Testament contains specific regulations and procedures the Jews were to follow in expressing their worship to God. These were meant to be a shadow of the real worship that comes from the heart, and the ceremonies and liturgies of the Old Testament were given to instruct people in something yet to be revealed. The New Testament offers a new revelation regarding the nature and purpose of worship. Let's review a conversation between Jesus and a woman of Samaria at an ancient well (keep in mind that Samaritans were half-Jewish and have half-Gentiles):

Jesus: "Would you draw Me a drink of water?"

Woman: "Why do You, a Jew, ask me, a Samaritan woman, for a drink? Your kind won't talk with Samaritans normally, and Your kind would never talk with a Samaritan woman."

Jesus: "If you understood how generous God is and who I am, you would be the one asking Me for a drink and I would give you water unlike anything you have ever had before."

Woman: "I'm confused—You don't have any bucket to draw water with, yet You say You would get me water? Are You better than Jacob, our ancestor who dug this well and passed it on to us?"

Jesus: "Everyone who drinks water from Jacob's well gets thirsty and has to keep on drawing more water, day after day. The water I give is like an artesian well inside of you and gushes fountains of life that last forever!"

Woman: "Sounds great to me! Give it to me so I don't have to keep coming back here day after day."

Jesus: "Go get your husband and come on back."

Woman: "I don't have a husband."

Jesus: "Interesting—you've had five husbands and you aren't married to the man you are living with now. So I guess you're right—you don't have a husband."

Woman: "Wow! How did You know that? You must be a prophet! Maybe You can answer a question for me: Our ancestors worshiped God on this mountain, but You 'pure' Jews insist that Jerusalem is the only acceptable place to worship God, right?"

Jesus: "Actually, real worship isn't going to happen on this mountain or in Jerusalem. But since you put it in that context, you worship with very little understanding, while the Jews have much more understanding about the nature of God. This is reflected in their ceremonies in Jerusalem. But the time has come when neither of these matter—now it's who you are and how you live your life that matter to God. God is looking for worshipers who will worship Him in spirit and in truth. This means He wants worship that is an intimate and honest interchange with people who love Him and who aren't simply performing some duty or ceremony."

Woman: "Well, at least I know that when the Messiah comes, He will explain all of this to us. We won't be confused any more when He comes."

Jesus: "Let me tell you something very special: I am the Messiah."

Can you imagine having this conversation with Jesus? What a shock—it still gives me goose bumps thinking about this woman's encounter with the Messiah. In the social order of the day, she would be near the bottom of the totem pole when being considered for a special meeting with God in the flesh. There are many insights to be gained from this interchange, but for our current pursuit of spiritual treasure, let's concentrate on the specific guidance Jesus offered about worship. His primary theme was that worship had become too formalized or institutionalized in Israel at that time and that God was looking for worshipers who would share an intimate, fully transparent relationship with Him. Jesus seemed to indicate that, though ritual offers some degree of enlightenment, heart-to-heart relationships of mutual love and intimacy are what God is seeking in worship.

So how can worship, in the context that Jesus was speaking of it, be considered a spiritual treasure? Worship is a diamond of the spirit because it comes from within us, rather than from some other source. It is a treasure from our spirit that can open up the unimaginable opportunity to share an intimate relationship with the Creator of the universe. Think about this for a moment—intimacy with the Creator of the universe! And in the process of experiencing this treasure beyond comprehension, worship brings additional treasures to the surface.

First, intimate worship gives us a more accurate perspective of reality. By nature, our lives are centered around us. Though we intellectually recognize this is delusionary, it is still how we respond in our time/space world. Worship helps to lift us out of this self-centered delusion and gives us glimpses of the true reality, that all of creation is centered on its Creator. In this way, worship helps us transcend our time/space boundaries to get a glimpse of the true center of all life and eternity.

Second, worship creates opportunities for divine intervention (or divine invasion) into our lives. As a result of worship, we become more aware of God's purpose and presence. We develop new sensitivities so that we recognize Him in situations that previously we took credit for ourselves or blamed on others. Worship brings us into the reality that God is big and wonderful enough to hold everything together, yet tender enough to take genuine interest in the minutest details of every single life. He is the ultimate macro- and micromanager, capable beyond our abilities to comprehend.

Third, worship changes us. Genuine, intimate worship and adoration for our Creator releases something in our spirit that finds its way into our soul (mind, will, emotions) and our body. Worship helps us to realize how far we fall short of God's character, wisdom, and righteousness, while at the same time drawing us into a personal revelation of how wonderful and all-encompassing His love and provision for us is. It is both scary and sacred at the same time. We are shocked and terrified when we see our own unrighteousness under the light of His presence, yet immeasurably comforted as we experience His love and compassion. Our times of worship in God's presence will create a noticeable change in who and what we are.

William Temple wrote, "To worship is to quicken the conscience by the holiness of God, to feed the mind with the truth of God, to purge the imagination by the beauty of God, to open the heart to the love of God, to devote the will to the purpose of God." With this in mind, there is a pattern of worship that helps us enter into God's presence. These steps into worship are not intended to form a new ritual. Instead, they help us to move away from self-consciousness and into God-consciousness as we go on a "date" with God:

1. Thanksgiving. Begin by thanking God for every good thing in your life. As you begin to quicken your spirit through thanksgiving, include giving thanks for the difficulties and disappointments also, because He works all things for your good. Thanksgiving can be expressed through verbal and physical expressions that may include singing, clapping, dancing, playing musical instruments, and reciting written declarations of thanksgiving. Some examples of thanksgiving in the Scriptures that you can use are Psalm 100, Psalm 107, 1

Chronicles 16:8–12, 1 Thessalonians 5:16–18, and 1 Chronicles 29:10–19.

2. Praise. Move from giving thanks for what God has done to giving Him praise for who He is. Praise is an expression of approval, esteem, or commendation. Once again, it can be expressed verbally, physically, and through artistic expression. If you play a musical instrument, or enjoy dancing or any other form of art, use your talent and desire to express God's nature. Some examples of praise in the Scriptures that you can use are 1 Chronicles 16:8–36 and Psalms 8, 34, 47, 103, 145, and 150.

3. Worship. Move from thanksgiving and praise into deeper adoration, reverence, and expressions of your love. It can be conveyed verbally through spontaneous expressions of devotion, poetry, and songs. It can be conveyed physically by kneeling, lifting up your hands, bowing your head, or lying flat on your stomach (prostrate) on the floor (or ground). The primary goal of worship at this point is to relate directly and intimately with God as a Person. Sometimes it is as simple as waiting quietly in His presence. Other times you may feel prompted to sing a love song to Him, or to write about your adoration of Him. Some examples of worship in the Bible are found in Exodus 33:5–8, 2 Chronicles 7:1–3, Psalm 63, and Revelations 4:6–11.

4. Silence. As you begin to experience God's Presence (through His Spirit), there will be times when you recognize Him taking the initiative and speaking to your heart. You may become aware of some way that you have failed and feel a need for confession and repentance, but the primary focus should be on listening. Learning to wait on God and practicing what author Dr. Mary Ruth Swope refers to as "Listening Prayer" will enrich your experience and release the "artesian well inside of you that gushes fountains of life" (see Psalm 27:14 and 46:10).

5. Recording. The ancients commemorated an encounter with God by building an altar of stones or by making a sacrifice. This helped to solidify the experience in their memory and created personal accountability to be true to their experience.

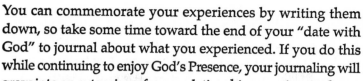

You can commemorate your experiences by writing them down, so take some time toward the end of your "date with God" to journal about what you experienced. If you do this while continuing to enjoy God's Presence, your journaling will grow into an extension of your relationship over time and new insights will come to you as you write.

6. Afterglow. As you move toward the end of your time of worship, continue to express praise and thanksgiving. I perceive this as backing out of the presence of the King rather than turning my back on Him and walking out of His presence without respect. The more respect and reverence you demonstrate, the higher the quality of your relationship will be over time.

7. Go and obey. Inevitably, your worship experiences will generate new inspiration for actions to take in your life. You complete the worship experience when you complete these actions. How will it affect your relationship with God if you receive wisdom and guidance and then don't follow through? On the other hand, imagine coming back into God's presence and being able to report to Him that you have completed the actions He gave you the last time you had fellowship together.

This pattern helps you to focus your relationship with God and unlocks continuous treasures of wisdom, strength, comfort, and renewal. However, worship can invade your life far beyond special times that you set aside to have a date with God. It's like my relationship with my wife. We are together every day, going about the many responsibilities of life. However, for our relationship to remain vibrant, we also need special times to be together, to focus on our relationship and intimate fellowship with one another, instead of always defining our relationship by the tasks that continually demand our attention. We pursue these special times through a dinner out, or a vacation away from the rest of our family, or just by taking a walk together. So, too, worship should be both a continual recognition of God's presence and friendship in your life, along with special times of worship when you can focus specifically on your relationship with one another.

Finally, true worship will lead you to expressing your love for God with lavish generosity. There are times when I want to do something "foolish" or lavish to express my love for my wife; the same desire should emerge in your relationship with God. The following story from Eugene Peterson's *The Message* illustrates this well:

> While Jesus was at Bethany, a guest of Simon the Leper, a woman came up to him as he was eating dinner and anointed him with a bottle of very expensive perfume. When the disciples saw what was happening, they were furious. "That's criminal! This could have been sold for a lot and the money handed out to the poor." When Jesus realized what was going on, he intervened. "Why are you giving this woman a hard time? She has just done something wonderfully significant for me. You will have the poor with you every day for the rest of your lives, but not me. When she poured this perfume on my body, what she really did was anoint me for burial. You can be sure that wherever in the whole world the Message is preached, what she has just done is going to be remembered and admired."

Most Bible scholars believe this bottle of perfume represented a full year's wages. It was a lavish expression that the disciples interpreted as foolish in light of the pressing needs around them. Jesus praised this woman for her discerning worship and adoration. If our experience with worship results in intimacy with the Almighty, similar expressions of lavish adoration will become a joy for us also.

Action Steps

1. Set aside one hour and have a date with God, using the pattern for worship in this chapter. Use the Scriptures noted to guide your experience. Write about your experience afterward and then schedule another date for the near future.

2. Arrive at your place of worship fifteen minutes before the

start of the service and prepare yourself by making a list of things that you are thankful for. Pray for those leading the service, asking for God's Spirit to lead them and bring the congregation into His presence. As people enter the service, choose one or two to pray for silently and pray for God's blessings to impact them both during the service and during the coming week. Seek to make your experience of this service more than the impersonal fulfillment of duty; may it become another genuine and intimate encounter with God.

3. Make a list of the attributes of God that are worthy of worship. Try to list at least twenty attributes and write a one-sentence description of what they mean in your life. Use this list for future worship experiences.

Points to Ponder

"To worship is to act as an inferior before a superior. When I worship God, I am saying by my actions, 'God, You are better than I am. You are bigger than I am. You are more than I am.'"
—Joseph L. Garlington, *Worship: The Pattern of Things in Heaven*

"One who knows God, worships God." — Anonymous

"Do you not know? Have you not heard? The LORD is the everlasting God, the Creator of the ends of the earth. He will not grow tired or weary, and his understanding no one can fathom. He gives strength to the weary and increases the power of the weak. Even youths grow tired and weary, and young men stumble and fall; but those who hope in the LORD will renew their strength. They will soar on wings like eagles; they will run and not grow weary, they will walk and not be faint."
— Isaiah 40:28–31

Chapter 29
Thanksgiving

Today upon a bus, I saw a lovely girl with golden hair.
I envied her, she seemed so gay, and wished I were as fair.
When suddenly she rose to leave, I saw her hobble down the aisle.
She had one leg and wore a crutch; but as she passed—a smile!
Oh, God, forgive me when I whine.
I have two legs, the world is mine.

And then I stopped to buy some candy. The lad who sold
them had such charm.
I talked with him, he seemed so glad. If I were late it would
do no harm.
And as I left, he said to me, "I thank you. You have been so kind.
You see," he said, "I am blind."
Oh, God, forgive me when I whine.
I have two eyes, the world is mine.

Later, when walking down the street, I saw a child with eyes
of blue.
He stood and watched the others play. He did not know
what to do.
I stopped a moment, then I said, "Why don't you join the
others, dear?"
He looked ahead without a word and then I knew, he could
not hear.
Oh, God, forgive me when I whine.
I have two ears, the world is mine.

With feet to take me where I'd go,
With eyes to see the sunset's glow,
With ears to hear what I would know,
Oh, God, forgive me when I whine,
I'm blessed indeed, the world is mine!
— Og Mandino

When we were kids, Thanksgiving meant lots of food, time

with my cousins, and professional football on a day other than Sunday (when I was a kid, there was no *Monday Night Football*). We learned that the holiday was about more than just getting together for a big meal. We learned the story of the Pilgrims who sailed to Plymouth Rock on Cape Cod in 1620. The Pilgrims' first Thanksgiving dinner was established to give thanks for their survival and to extend friendship to the local Wampanoag Indians. But to give thanks for what? In their first year, the Pilgrims lost forty-seven of the ninety-nine who sailed due to illness and the harsh conditions. All but three families lost loved ones, and thirteen of the eighteen mothers who crossed the Atlantic died. In spite of this seemingly unbearable suffering, they gathered to give thanks.

What strength of character it must have taken to be thankful in the midst of so much suffering. In order for us to be thankful in modern America, most of us need our thermostat adjusted just right, our refrigerator full, and our favorite television program on. And, of course, the kids need to be quiet. Yet these Pilgrims, with so few possessions and so much suffering, gathered to give thanks for the Providence that brought them through their first winter in the New World.

Quite often I drive by my chiropractor's office. As so many businesses do, he has a reader board with various messages posted on it from time to time. One November he posted a message that sticks with me still today: "He who is thankful for little, enjoys much!"

Watching the way people interact with each other, I have discovered something very interesting: quite often, we try to get attention by complaining. In spite of this habit, I have noticed that other people prefer to be around someone who is thankful more than someone who is complaining. I have noticed that most people are starved for some genuine appreciation. And I have noticed that I change when I cultivate a habit of giving thanks at every opportunity. It is almost impossible to be thankful and complaining at the same time. One or the other has to go, so if you focus on thanksgiving, much of the misery of life disappears. When you fill up your mind with thanksgiving, it's not comfortable hanging around someone with a critical and negative attitude. I have also noticed that almost every problem begins to shrink in size when my life is permeated with thanksgiving.

So why aren't more of us thankful? Because it isn't easy. In our nature, we find it easier to look for the greener grass on the other side of the fence, to blame circumstances and other people for our unhappiness and disappointments, and to compare ourselves with others by looking for their faults in an attempt to boost our self-esteem. We may attempt to find happiness by changing friends, commitments, and locations, only to find that it takes just a short time for misery to return—because we bring it with us!

H. W. Beecher wrote about thankfulness and had some interesting commentary:

> If one should give me a dish of sand, and tell me there were particles of iron in it, I might look for them with my eyes, and search for them with my clumsy fingers, and be unable to detect them; but let me take a magnet and sweep through it, and how would it draw to itself the almost invisible particles by the mere power of attraction. The unthankful heart, like my finger in the sand, discovers no mercies; but let the thankful heart sweep through the day, and as the magnet finds the iron, so it will find, in every hour, some heavenly blessings, only the iron in God's sand is gold!
>
> Pride slays thanksgiving, but a humble mind is the soil out of which thanks naturally grow. A proud man is seldom a grateful man, for he never thinks he gets as much as he deserves.

The connection between pride and ingratitude is profound. Can we assume that whenever we succumb to whining we are also exposing an unhealthy pride, and that one of the greatest weapons we have against ugly pride is thankfulness? I think so—and there are many promises in the Scriptures for the humble woman or man:

When pride comes, then comes disgrace, but with humility comes wisdom. (Proverbs 11:2)

The fear of the LORD teaches a man wisdom, and humility comes before honor. (Proverbs 15:33)

Humility and the fear of the LORD bring wealth and honor and life. (Proverbs 22:4)

All of you, clothe yourselves with humility toward one another, because, "God opposes the proud but gives grace to the humble." Humble yourselves, therefore, under God's mighty hand, that he may lift you up in due time. (1 Peter 5:5–6)

I have spoken and written about thanksgiving many times over the years. Yet it was in the writing of this chapter that I saw the direct connection between thankfulness, humility, and the fear of God for the first time. In counseling sessions, people often acknowledge pride and reckless living and ask for guidance about how to change what seem to be unbreakable patterns. The answer is thanksgiving. To the extent that we become truly thankful (and it is a habit, not a talent), we become genuinely humble and respectful of God and others. If they are anything, pride and reckless living are the fruit of a tree that has a taproot of ingratitude. It should become the top priority of our daily living to increase our thanksgiving, because genuine thankfulness opens up so many other treasures in our lives.

Action Steps

1. Spend at least thirty minutes making a list of everything you own. You probably won't capture everything in thirty minutes, but in creating this list you will realize that even the poorest among us lives an abundant life. You also will have a list to use in giving thanks. (This is also good to do as a family— put a large poster board up on the refrigerator door and have each family member add one item to be thankful for each

morning or evening until you have filled up the poster board
completely.)

2. Spend at least thirty minutes making a list of everyone you
know. Again, you will probably not get everyone on the list in
thirty minutes, but the exercise of writing their names will
increase your gratitude for the relationships you have. As a
result, you may decide to reconnect with some friends you
have lost touch with.

3. Spend at least thirty minutes making a list of every talent or
ability you have. (Most of us will finish this exercise early
because we suffer from low self-esteem.) Think of all the hidden
treasures we have reviewed in this book, as well as special
talents and skills you may have in the arts, athletics, or the
sciences. Once again, this list will give you much to be thankful
for as well as stir some inspiration about how to use your
talents and skills more effectively.

Points to Ponder

> Think of things that make you happy,
> Not the things that make you sad;
> Think of the fine and true in mankind,
> Not its sordid side and bad;
> Think of the blessings that surround you,
> Not the ones that are denied;
> Think of the virtues of your friendships,
> Not the weak and faulty side;
>
> Think of the gains you've made in business,
> Not the losses that you've incurred;
> Think of the good of you that's spoken,
> Not some cruel, hostile word;
> Think of the days of health and pleasure,
> Not the days of woe and pain;
> Think of the days alive with sunshine,
> Not the dismal days of rain;

Think of the hopes that lie before you,
Not the waste that lies behind;
Think of the treasures you have gathered,
Not the ones you've failed to find;
Think of the service you may render,
Not of serving self alone;
Think of the happiness of others,
And in this you'll find your own!
— Robert E. Farley

Chapter 30
Giving

Power is a resource that allows us to move from one condition of reality to another. It provides the opportunity to improve some aspect of our lives, either in comfort, in illumination, or in achievement.

For many pages, we have been looking at sources of personal power. These inner resources for producing change in our lives are mysterious, both because of their universal availability, and because more often than not they remain dormant within us. These inner resources are similar to a mine of precious diamonds. They appear plain, common, and of minimal value at first glance, yet they represent the most precious part of life when properly mined and polished.

Most people are in the habit of attributing power to circumstances, to others, and to fate. We fall short of our hopes and abandon our dreams, blaming the economy, the government, painful and dysfunctional childhoods, abuse from teachers and employers, or maybe for no other reason than being caught in a whirlwind of change and activity that steals our sense of purpose and control. Yet the inner treasures of power still remain, crying out from deep within, imploring that we might discover and employ them for a brighter, more dynamic and fulfilling future.

Think about the topics you have read about to this point. Treasures of the mind, treasures of the heart, treasures of the body, and treasures of the spirit. Success, prosperity, fulfillment, and happiness don't come from the latest business opportunity, your rich uncle, or a winning lottery ticket. The highest and noblest achievement in life always come from tapping into these resources of hidden treasures and releasing the latent power within.

To complete our look at diamonds of the spirit, I would like to share with you one more hidden treasure I have discovered that is inseparable from lasting achievement and fulfillment. This final treasure, available to all of us, is the treasure of giving.

Henry Emerson Fosdick, a favorite author of my grandfather, wrote in 1920, "The Sea of Galilee and the Dead Sea are made of the same water. It flows down, clear and cool, from the heights of Hermon and the roots of the cedars of Lebanon. The Sea of Galilee makes beauty of it, for the Sea of Galilee has an outlet. It gets to give. It gathers in its riches that it may pour them out again to fertilize the Jordan plain. But the Dead Sea with the same water makes horror. For the Dead Sea has no outlet. It gets to keep."

What is this strange law of nature, that power is generated in giving rather than in getting? John Bunyan wrote, "There was a man, though some did count him mad, the more he cast away the more he had." The Chinese writer Lao-Tzu wrote, "The sage does not accumulate for himself. The more he uses for others, the more he possesses of his own. The way of Heaven is to benefit others and not to injure."

John D. Rockefeller, one of the wealthiest men in American history, spent a good portion of his life getting and accumulating. He was known as a tough, sometimes ruthless businessman. Yet his accumulation of wealth, political power, and reputation didn't bring peace or contentment. In his later years, he discovered the truth in Henry Drummond's statement that real happiness is in giving rather than getting. He made giving his number one priority, and the Rockefeller Foundation continues as one of the most generous philanthropic organizations today, more than seven decades after his death. (I confess that I am often at odds with the causes the Foundation supports. However, no one can deny the example of generosity it continues to demonstrate in the spirit of its founder.) I believe John D. Rockefeller has been much maligned by those who have written about him. Not understanding the depth of his conversion, they accused him of giving to relieve a guilty conscience. However, a closer and more discerning investigation would reveal a man who discovered one of the greatest secrets of life—the power of giving!

The Scriptures also have plenty to say about the treasure of giving:

> Trust in the LORD with all your heart and lean not on your own understanding; in all your ways acknowledge him, and he will make your paths straight. Do not be wise in your own eyes; fear the LORD and shun evil. This will bring health to your body and nourishment to your bones. Honor the LORD from your wealth, with the firstfruits of all your crops; then your barns will be filled to overflowing, and your vats will brim over with new wine. (Proverbs 3:5–10)

> He who gives to the poor will lack nothing, but he who closes his eyes to them receives many curses. (Proverbs 28:27)

> Give, and it will be given unto you. A good measure, pressed down, shaken together and running over, will be poured into your lap. For with the measure you use, it will be measured to you. (Luke 6:38)

> Remember this: Whoever sows sparingly will also reap sparingly, and whoever sows generously will also reap generously. Each man should give what he has decided in his heart to give, not reluctantly or under compulsion, for God loves a cheerful giver. (2 Corinthians 9:6–7)

Here are some suggestions for releasing the full power of giving in your life:

First, give early and give often. He who is not generous with what he has should not deceive himself that he would be generous if he had more. No matter where you find yourself today, find some way to give. Don't worry about how much or how little; just start giving. Longfellow wrote, "Give what you have. To some one it may be better than you dare to think." Let me share one caution, however: Give without going into debt, for most of the joy in giving is lost when it results in a charge card bill you can't pay next month. Instead of empowering you as giving is intended to do, indebtedness steals from your future and perverts the power of giving. You don't need to have large reserves of money to cultivate the power of giving. You can give time, energy, emotional support, and material possessions. Giving early and often nurtures an attitude that creates a larger and larger capacity for you to receive.

Second, give to those who cannot give in return. One of the great promises in the Bible is that he who gives to the poor lends to their Maker. And I'm confident He pays His debts with an attractive interest rate! John Wesley wrote, "The more good we do, the happier we shall be. The more we deal our bread to the hungry, and cover the naked with garments; the more we relieve the stranger, and visit them that are sick or in prison; the more kind offices we do to those that groan under the various evils of human life, the more comfort we receive even in the present world; the greater the recompense we have in our own bosom." Giving to those who cannot give in return is a key to releasing the power of giving in your life.

Third, give to those who oppose you. This is understandably one of the most difficult giving disciplines to cultivate. But it may have more inherent power than any other kind of giving in life. When we learn generosity with our enemies, we develop a depth of giving that reflects the Divine. The apostle Paul captured the essence of this giving power when he wrote, "God demonstrates his own love for us in this: While we were still sinners, Christ died for us" (Romans 5:8). In Jesus' famous Sermon on the Mount—which I believe is one of the all-time greatest treatises on personal power—He told His followers, "You have heard that it was said, 'Love your neighbor and hate your enemy.' But I tell you: Love your enemies and pray for those who persecute you, that you may be sons of your Father in heaven. He causes his sun to rise on the evil and the good, and sends rain on the righteous and the unrighteous" (Matthew 5:43–45). When the power of giving has matured in us so much that we can cheerfully give to those who oppose us, the kingdom of heaven is not far away.

Giving is an attitude, a treasure of the spirit. When you uncover it in your life, resources will begin to flow to you in greater and greater quantities and you will find the reality of Jesus' declaration, "It is more blessed to give than to receive." For you cannot out-give God.

Action Steps

1. Examine your attitude toward giving. Do you give out of duty or out of joy? Are you praying for and finding ways to give what you have (money, possessions, time, energy, emotional support)? Write out some goals for how you can increase your giving over the next month and the next year.

2. Begin your giving by honoring God. Ask Him to speak to your spirit to show you where and how to give according to His pleasure. Give at least ten percent of your income as soon as you receive it as an expression of thanks to God. (For more on the power of this giving, visit www.lifequestintl.com.)

3. Find small ways to give something to others in need every week. As giving becomes part of your weekly focus, your generosity and resources will begin to increase. Here are some suggestions for giving:

> a. Become active, both financially and through volunteering, in a local service club, such as Rotary, Kiwanis, or Lions.
>
> b. Look for people in need and then find ways to give anonymously to assist them.
>
> c. Take someone to lunch whom you admire and insist on paying for his lunch as a way of recognizing this person's value and contribution in your life.
>
> d. Take someone to lunch whom you have struggled with or are experiencing conflict with. Tell him what you genuinely appreciate about him (pay for his lunch also).

Points to Ponder

"There is no happiness in having or getting, but only in giving. Half of the world is on the wrong scent in the pursuit of happiness. They think it consists of having and getting and in being served by others. It consists of giving and serving others."
— Henry Drummond, author

"A committed giver is an incurably happy person, a secure person, a satisfied person, and a prosperous person." — Eric Butterworth, author, theologian, philosopher

"What I kept I lost.
What I spent I had.
What I gave I have."
           — Persian proverb

Staking Your Claim For Hidden Treasures

In the gold rush days of the mid-to-late 1800s, thousands and thousands of people responded to a dream for instant wealth by taking risks far beyond what most of us could imagine today. People braving the Western frontiers in search of hidden treasure populated California, Alaska, Idaho, Montana, Nevada, New Mexico, South Dakota, Utah, and Wyoming. From 1851 to 1890, Australia's population almost tripled because of people in search of gold, and New Zealand's population doubled during the next seven years. South Africa and Canada experienced similar gold rushes in the late 1800s.

The vast majority of those who left home and family in search of gold, however, never found the object of their dreams. A very small percentage fulfilled their quest for instant wealth, while a much larger number eventually came to grips with their failure to achieve that and found other ways to settle into new surroundings and build a life of purpose and some degree of prosperity. For some, the failure to strike it rich was devastating and their lives were ruined, never to recover.

The search for treasures can be a risky business—yet the treasures still exist, waiting to be discovered. Even after one hundred and fifty years, there is still unclaimed gold in the hills of the western United States, as well as every other country where a gold rush has occurred. There are still an immeasurable number of diamonds waiting to be unearthed in Africa, India, Russia and South America. The issue is never the depletion of resources. Instead, it always comes back to the value we place on hidden treasures and our willingness to risk and sacrifice in the pursuit of our dreams (which is the primary reason gold prospecting has lost its luster today—the cost of finding and mining gold is rarely justified when compared with its perceived value).

How about you? Are you satisfied with what you have and who you are? Are you content to live with what you have discovered so far in your life, knowing that there are limitless resources within your mind, heart, body, and spirit? Is it okay with you to leave your hidden treasures untouched because the risk and sacrifice would force you out of your current comfort zone? Or are you an adventurer, hungry to discover more about yourself and to unearth as much treasure as possible during your short journey through life?

At some point each of us has aspired to some kind of greatness. Not a greatness defined by the world around us necessarily, but a greatness that we feel and define from deep within. Something or someone touches us in a way that makes us say, "I want to be _____" or, "I want to do _____ before my life is over." For some of us it is a role model who impacts us early in life. This unique person inspires us at a formative time to want to be like him or her when we grow up and to imitate the greatness we feel in that person's presence. For others it is a reaction to something negative we experience. The pain we feel motivates us to vow we will take another course and pay whatever price is necessary to avoid replicating the negative experience or relationship that has shown us the hard side of life. It doesn't matter which type of experience ignites our aspiration for greatness, only how we respond to the challenge.

Unfortunately, far too many people trade this hunger for greatness somewhere along life's path for what they perceive as a more secure existence of mediocrity and self-protection. Some of us compromise our deep dreams because of personal failures. We disappoint ourselves and lose confidence in our ability to overcome the obstacles that confront us at various junctures in our journey. We also may give up our adventures because of a sense of obligation to others who will be hurt if the risks are too high. And some give up on the pursuit of a higher and nobler purpose because of a gradual slide into cynicism about life, human nature, and what the ancient Greeks called "fate." Yet if we listen closely enough, the yearning for greatness still cries out from deep within our souls, because it is an undeniable part of life itself.

Do you remember when this call to greatness first revealed itself within your consciousness? Do you remember the experience that brought you the dream that is special for you alone? Some of us discover it in our youth; for others we have to experience more of life before it emerges. For me, this sense of destiny is reawakened during a special time of reflection, or while listening to another person share about the greatness he has discovered for his own life. When he begins to open up his heart and share the treasures of his life, a chord is struck within me that brings the deep desire to spend my life in service to others, to experience and reflect the glory of God. It is a power so great that it transcends my own needs or wants and encompasses me with the joy of giving my life for something much greater than self-gratification.

It doesn't matter how many years have passed since you first felt the tug toward greatness. It doesn't matter if you let the flame burn low somewhere along the way. No matter what your history, there is still a flicker of this quest for greatness alive in you today. In spite of discouragement, failure, or misplaced ambitions, it still flickers deep within you. It lives in you because it is a gift from God and is the fundamental substance that makes you so much more important than you probably realize.

What if you chose, once again, to respond to this call to greatness? How do you take the first step? "A journey of a thousand miles begins with a single step." This Chinese proverb has become cliché, yet it is still profound in its truth. That first step is always a step of faith, into the unknown. It is a willingness to believe in what cannot be seen, for all who aspire to greatness must "walk by faith, not by sight" (2 Corinthians 5:7, KJV).

In a certain sense, greatness is timeless. It doesn't matter what your age is, where you have already been, or what degree of success or failure you have already experienced. You can learn from the past, both good and bad, but you can no longer live there. What is done is done, and if you become imprisoned to either the good or the bad that you have done, you forfeit what life still holds for you to embrace.

You can look to the future and help to create the path you will walk on to some extent through your optimism and passion, choosing the best and climbing over the worst that happens along the way. But it is still only a forecast of what may be in the future, not yet a reality that you can depend on for happiness and fulfillment.

You can truly achieve greatness only in the present, because that is where you take action to express the aspirations that bring forth your hidden treasures. It is in the present that you love, you overcome, and you serve people and a purpose higher than yourself. This means that today is the day for you to respond to the unlimited hidden treasures within. Today is the day for you to cast off the disappointment of past failures and turn your heart toward new opportunities. Today is the day to offer your assistance to someone else in need, to begin the creation of a new habit that you know will set you on the path to fulfilling the secret dreams that will ignite your heart, engage your mind, and invigorate you with energy and strength. Today is the day to stake your claim and start finding your hidden treasures!

The Race
by D. H. Groberg

I.

"Quit! Give up! You're beaten!"
They shout at me and plead.
"There's just too much against you now.
This time you can't succeed!"

And as I start to hang my head
In front of failure's face,
My downward fall is broken by
The memory of a race.

And hope refills my weakened will
As I recall that scene;
For just the thought of that short race
Rejuvenates my being.

II.

A children's race—young boys, young men
How I remember well.
Excitement, sure! But also fear;
It wasn't hard to tell.

They all lined up so full of hope;
Each thought to win that race.
Or tie for first, or if not that,
At least take second place.

And fathers watched from off the side,
Each cheering for his son.
And each boy hoped to show his dad
That he would be the one.

The whistle blew and off they went!
Young hearts and hopes afire.
To win and be the hero there
Was each young boy's desire.

And one boy in particular
Whose dad was in the crowd,
Was running near the lead and thought,
"My dad will be so proud!"

But as they speeded down the field
Across a shallow dip,
The little boy who thought to win
Lost his step and slipped.

Trying hard to catch himself
His hands flew out to brace,
And mid the laughter of the crowd
He fell flat on his face.

So down he fell and with him hope
He couldn't win it now—
Embarrassed, sad, he only wished
To disappear somehow.

But as he fell his dad stood up
And showed his anxious face,
Which to the boy so clearly said:
"Get up and win the race."

He quickly rose, no damage done.
Behind a bit, that's all—
And ran with all his mind and might
To make up for his fall.

So anxious to restore himself
To catch up and to win—
His mind went faster than his legs;
He slipped and fell again!

He wished then he had quit before
With only one disgrace.
"I'm hopeless as a runner now;
I shouldn't try to race."

But in the laughing crowd he searched
And found his father's face.
That steady look which said again:
"Get up and win the race!"

So up he jumped to try again
Ten yards behind the last—
"If I'm to gain those yards," he thought,
"I've got to move real fast."

Exerting everything he had
He gained eight or ten
But trying so hard to catch the lead
He slipped and fell again!

Defeat! He lay there silently
A tear dropped from his eye—
"There's no sense running any more:
Three strikes: I'm out! Why try?"

The will to rise had disappeared
All hope had fled away;
So far behind, so error prone;
A loser all the way.

"I've lost, so what's the use," he thought.
"I'll live with my disgrace."
But then he thought about his dad
Who soon he'd have to face.

"Get up," an echo sounded low.
"Get up and take your place;
You were not meant for failure here.
Get up and win the race."

"With borrowed will, get up," it said,
"You haven't lost at all,
For winning is no more than this:
To rise each time you fall."

So up he rose to run once more,
And with a new commit
He resolved that win or lose
At least he wouldn't quit.

So far behind the others now,
The most he'd ever been—
Still he gave it all he had
And ran as though to win.

Three times he'd fallen, stumbling;
Three times he rose again;
Too far behind to hope to win
He still ran to the end.

They cheered the winning runner
As he crossed the line first place,
Head high, and proud, and happy;
No falling, no disgrace.

But when the youngster
Crossed the line last place,
The crowd gave him the greater cheer
For finishing the race.

And even though he came in last
With head bowed low, unproud,
You would have thought he'd won the
Race to listen to the crowd.

And to his dad he sadly said,
"I didn't do so well."
"To me, you won," his father said.
"You rose each time you fell."

III.
And now when things seem dark and hard
And difficult to face,
The memory of that little boy
Helps me in my own race.

For all of life is like that race,
With ups and downs and all.
And all you have to do to win,
Is rise each time you fall.

"Quit! Give up! You're beaten!"
They still shout in my face.
But another voice within me says:
"GET UP AND WIN THE RACE!"

Alexander, A. L. *Poems That Touch the Heart*. New York: Doubleday, 1956.

Allen, James. *As a Man Thinketh*. Mechanicsburg, Pa.: Life Management Services, 1983.

The Amplified Bible. Grand Rapids, Mich.: Zondervan Publishing House, 1965.

Batmanghelidj, F., M.D. *Your Body's Many Cries for Water*. Falls Church, Va.: Global Health Solutions, 1997.

The Book, New Living Translation. Wheaton, Ill.: Tyndale House Publishers, 1996.

Bragg, Patricia, Ph.D. *Bragg Super Power Breathing*. Santa Barbara, Calif.: Health Science, (publishing date unknown)

Bragg, Patricia, Ph.D. *The Shocking Truth about Water*. Santa Barbara, Calif.: Health Science, 1983.

Carnegie, Dale. *How to Win Friends and Influence People*. New York: Simon & Schuster, 1981.

Chambers, Oswald. *My Utmost for His Highest*. Westwood, N.J.: Oswald Chambers Publications Association, 1963.

Clark, Thomas. *1000 Quotable Poems*. Chicago: Willett, Clark & Company, 1937.

Contreras, Francisco, M.D. *Health in the 21st Century*. Chula Vista, Calif.: Interpacific Press, 1997.

Conwell, Russell. *Modern Eloquence, Volume VIII*. New York, London: Modern Eloquence Corporation, 1923.

Covey, Stephen. *The Seven Habits of Highly Effective People*. New

York: Simon & Schuster, 1989.

Doan, Eleanor. *The Complete Speakers Sourcebook*. Grand Rapids, Mich.: Zondervan Publishing, 1996.

Dyet, Jim, and Russell, Jim. *Overcoming Subtle Sins*. Lansing, Mich.: The Amy Foundation, 2002.

Edwards, Tyron, D.D. *The New Dictionary of Thoughts*. New York: Standard Book Company, 1936.

Exline, Eric. *The Healthy Cell Concept*. Nampa, Idaho: AIM International, 1995.

Ehret, Arnold. *Mucusless Diet Healing System*. Dobbs Ferry, N.Y.: Ehret Literature Publishing, 1983.

Foster, Richard J. *Celebration of Discipline: The Path to Spiritual Growth*. San Francisco: Harper & Row, 1978

Fuller, Edmund. *2500 Anecdotes for All Occasions*. New York: Crown Publishers, 1970.

Garlington, Joseph L. *Right or Reconciled? God's Heart for Reconciliation*. Shippensburg, Pa.: Destiny Image Publishers, 1998.

Garlington, Joseph L. *Worship: The Pattern of Things in Heaven*. Shippensburg, Pa.: Destiny Image Publishers, 1997.

Griffith, Joe. *Speaker's Library of Business Stories, Anecdotes and Humor*. Englewood Cliffs, N.J.: Prentice-Hall, 1990.

Hagiwara, Yoshihide, M.D. *Green Barley Essence*. New Canaan, Conn.: Keats Publishing, 1985.

Hill, Napoleon. *Think & Grow Rich*. Meriden, Conn.: The Ralston Society, 1944.

Hill, Napoleon, and Stone, W. Clement. *Success through a*

Positive Mental Attitude. New York: Simon & Schuster, 1987.

Howell, Edward. *Enzyme Nutrition: The Food Enzyme Concept*. Wayne, N.J.: Avery Publishing, 1985.

Jones, Charlie "Tremendous". *Life Is Tremendous*. Mechanicsburg, Pa.: Executive Books, 1968.

Kohe, J. Martin. *Your Greatest Power*. Cleveland, Ohio: The Ralston Publishing Company, 1953.

Lee, John R., M.D. *What Your Doctor May Not Tell You about Menopause*. New York: Warner Books, 1996.

Lenarz, Michael, D.C. *The Chiropractic Way*. New York: Bantam Books, 2003.

Malkmus, George, Rev. *Why Christians Get Sick*. Shippensburg, Pa.: Destiny Image Publishers, 1989.

Maltz, Maxwell, M.D., F.I.C.S. *Psycho-Cybernetics*. New York: Simon & Schuster, 1960.

Mandino, Og. *The Greatest Miracle in the World*. New York: Bantam Books, 1975.

Mandino, Og. *Og Mandino's University of Success*. New York: Bantam Books, 1982.

Mendelsohn, Robert S., M.D. *Confessions of a Medical Heretic*. New York: Warner Books, 1979.

Maxwell, John C. *The 21 Irrefutable Laws of Leadership*. Nashville, Tenn.: Thomas Nelson Publishers, 1998.

The New Chain-Reference Bible, King James Version. Indianapolis, Ind.: BB. Kirkbride Bible Co, 1964.

Packer, Lester, Ph.D., and Colman, Carol. *The Antioxidant Miracle*. New York: John Wiley & Sons, 1999.

Peale, Norman Vincent. *The Power of Positive Thinking.* New York: Fawcett Columbine, 1952.

Peck, M. Scott, M.D. *The Road Less Traveled.* New York: Simon & Schuster, 1978.

Peterson, Eugene H. *The Message: The New Testament in Contemporary Language.* Colorado Springs, Colo.: NavPress, 1994.

Phillips, Bill. *Body for Life.* New York: HarperCollins Publishers, 1999.

Platt, Suzy. *Respectfully Quoted: A Dictionary of Quotations.* New York: Barnes & Noble Books, 1993.

Prince, Derek. *The Spirit-Filled Believer's Handbook.* Lake Mary, Fla.: Charisma House, 1993.

Richardson, Cheryl. *Stand Up for Your Life.* New York: The Free Press, 2002.

Roach, Geshe Michael. *The Diamond Cutter.* New York: Doubleday, 2000.

Santillo, Humbart, B.S., M.H. *Natural Healing with Herbs.* Prescott Valley, Ariz.: Hohm Press, 1984.

Schuller, Robert H. *The Be-Happy Attitudes.* Waco, Tex.: Word Books, 1985.

Schumacher, Teresa, & Lund, Toni. *Cleansing the Body and the Colon for a Happier and Healthier You.* St. George, Utah: Teresa Schumacher, 1996.

Siegel, Bernie S., M.D. *Love, Medicine & Miracles.* New York: Harper & Row, 1986.

Sinatra, Stephen, M.D. *Optimum Health.* New York: Bantam Books, 1996.

Spinard, Leonard & Spinard, Thelma. *Speaker's Lifetime Library.* West Nyack, N.Y.: Parker Publishing Company, 1979.

Stanko, John, Ph.D. *Life Is a Goldmine, Can You Dig It?* Mobile, Ala.: Evergreen Press, 1995.

Stanley, Paul D., and Clinton, J. Robert. *Connecting.* Colorado Springs, Colo.: NavPress, 1992.

Swope, Dr. Mary Ruth. *Green Leaves of Barley.* Phoenix, Ariz.: Swope Enterprises, 1990.

Van Ekeren, Glenn. *Speaker's Sourcebook II.* Englewood Cliffs, N.J.: Prentice-Hall, 1994.

Van Ekeren, Glenn. *Words for All Occasions.* Englewood Cliffs, N.J.: Prentice-Hall, 1988.

Walker, Norman, D.Sc., Ph.D. *Colon Health: The Key to a Vibrant Life.* Prescott, Ariz.: Norwalk Press, 1979.

Walker, Norman, D.Sc., Ph.D. *Fresh Vegetable and Fruit Juices.* Prescott, Ariz.: Norwalk Press, 1970.

Willard, Dallas. *The Spirit of the Disciplines: Understanding How God Changes Lives.* San Francisco: HarperCollins, 1988.

Index